The Art of
HAND
READING

The Art of
HAND
READING

LORI REID

TO FRASER, SOPHIE AND ALASDAIR
WITH LOVE

A DK PUBLISHING BOOK

PROJECT EDITOR TRACIE LEE
ART EDITOR KEVIN RYAN
MANAGING EDITOR FRANCIS RITTER
MANAGING ART EDITOR DEREK COOMBES
DTP DESIGNER CRESSIDA JOYCE
PRODUCTION CONTROLLER RUTH CHARLTON
US EDITOR BETH IOGHA

•

First American Edition 1996
2 4 6 8 10 9 7 5 3 1

Published in the United States by DK Publishing, Inc.,
95 Madison Avenue, New York, New York 10016
Visit us on the World Wide Web at http://www.dk.com

Copyright © 1996 Dorling Kindersley Limited, London

Text copyright © 1996 Lori Reid

The right of Lori Reid to be identified as
Writer of this Work has been asserted
by her in accordance with the Copyright, Designs,
and Patents Act 1988.

All rights reserved under International and Pan-American
Copyright Conventions. No part of this publication may be
reproduced, stored in a retrieval system, or transmitted in
any form or by any means, electronic, mechanical,
photocopying, recording, or otherwise, without the prior
written permission of the copyright owner. Published in
Great Britain by Dorling Kindersley Limited.
Distributed by Houghton Mifflin Company, Boston.

Library of Congress Cataloging-in Publication Data
Reid, Lori.
    The art of hand reading / by Lori Reid.
    p.   cm.
    Includes index.
    ISBN 0–7894–1060–5
    1. Palmistry. I. Title.
BF921. R42 1996   96–15506
133.6 – dc20   CIP

Reproduced by Scanner Service, Italy
Printed and bound in Great Britain by
Butler and Tanner

CONTENTS

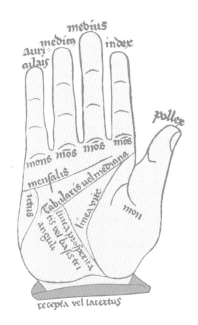

INTRODUCTION 7

THE HAND 23

The Lines 51

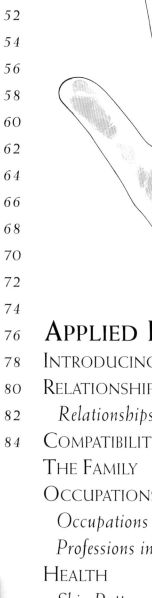

Applied Hand Analysis 87

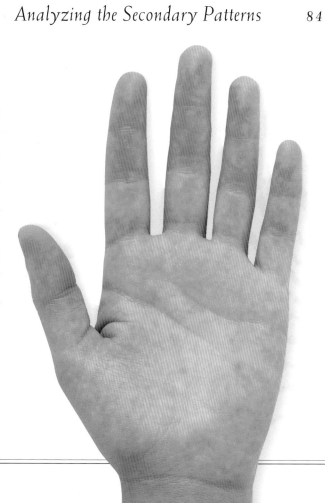

INTRODUCTION

·

The art of hand reading has evolved over thousands of years, from Stone Age man's curiosity to the sophisticated techniques of today's practitioner. Our growing understanding of genetics coupled with modern scientific procedures is opening a new chapter in hand analysis, for we are beginning to recognize that the patterns in our hands are a blueprint of our physical and psychological selves.

A LOOK AT THE HAND • INTRODUCING
THE HAND • THE HISTORY OF HAND
READING • THE HAND IN COMMUNICATION
THE ANATOMY OF THE HAND

A LOOK AT THE HAND

EACH OF US BELIEVES we are familiar with our own hands, and we tend to take them for granted and use them automatically. It is not until we examine our hands critically that we begin to appreciate the many interesting features that they actually possess. To understand and analyze your own hands you must look at each component in turn: the shape and structure of the palm, the length and build of the fingers, the strength and flexibility of the thumb, the size and construction of the nails, the pattern and composition of the skin ridges, and the quality and formation of the lines in the palm.

Each of these features in your hand, whether by its construction, shape, color, temperature, or other characteristic, will reveal information about your character and personality, about your likes and dislikes, about your motivations and desires,

and about how you see the world and live your life. Analyzing each of these features in turn will give you deeper insights into yourself and will enable you to piece together, rather like a jigsaw puzzle, a complete personality profile of you.

FINGERTIPS AND PHALANXES
The shape of your fingertips reveals how you express your talents to the outside world. The length and thickness of the phalanxes pinpoint your special abilities. See page 38.

THE FINGERS
Each finger represents a particular facet of life. Its shape and construction highlights the importance you place on that aspect in your own life. See page 36.

THE FINGERNAILS
The fingernails are invaluable for judging the state of your health. The color of the nails, the appearance of the moons, and the condition of the nail itself are all useful diagnostic aids. Psychologically, the shape and size of the fingernails are associated with specific character traits that help to build a full personality profile. See pages 44, 108.

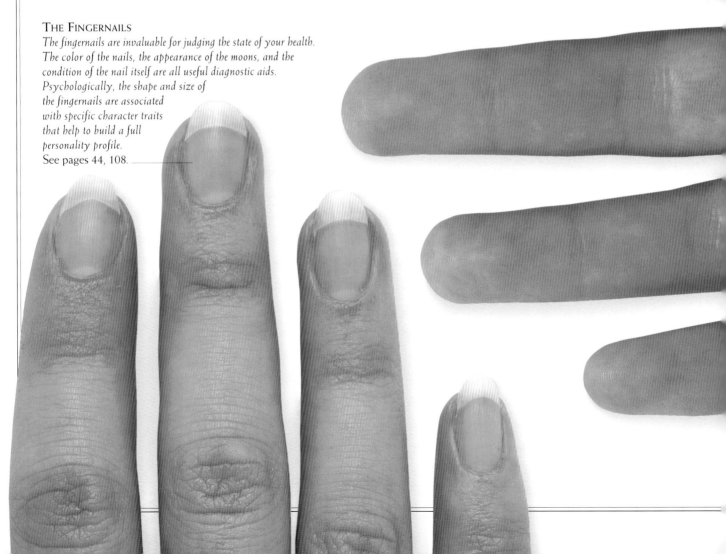

THE THUMB
The most important of all the digits, your thumb reveals whether you have the determination to bring your talents to fruition. See page 40.

THE PALM
The richest concentration of information about yourself lies in your palms. The construction of this area contains clues to your physical and psychological makeup, while the formation of the lines provides insights into your character strengths and weaknesses. Additionally, your lines record past events and reveal patterns of future trends. See pages 26, 30, 52.

THE MOUNTS
The nine padded areas around the palm are called mounts. Each one is associated with a different aspect of your personality. See page 30.

THE MAJOR LINES
The major lines comprise the life, head, heart, fate, and Apollo lines. Each one represents a specific area of your life and describes characteristics and events that are associated with it. See page 52.

THE SECONDARY LINES
Lines that are additional to the major lines are known as secondary lines and add further depth and interest to the character profile. See page 82.

PALMAR RIDGE PATTERNS
The palm side of your hand is covered by skin stamped with ridges and furrows that flow, sometimes in parallel lines, sometimes in the familiar patterns we recognize as fingerprints. These patterns give important clues about your character and genetic inheritance. See page 48.

INTRODUCING THE HAND

THE HANDS are the most flexible and complex part of the human body. With our hands we manipulate our environment and accomplish millions of intricate actions every day; we take care of essential physical necessities of life, we express ourselves artistically and musically, and construct the world around us. Indeed, our evolutionary survival and success as a race are attributable to the fact that as human beings we have hands with opposing thumbs that enable us to grip.

Anatomically, the hands are so important that a greater proportion of the brain is dedicated to them than to any other part of the body. Of the approximately two hundred million nerve fibers that make up the brain, a disproportionately large

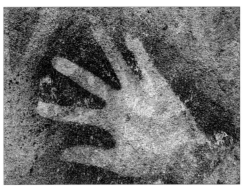

HAND STENCILS
The hand stencils on the walls of the Wargata Mina Cave in southwestern Tasmania are 15,000 years old. The stencils of the left and right hands of five people were made by blowing a spray of powdered pigment mixed with water over the hands. They may have been associated with initiation rituals or visits by elders.

amount are dedicated to the hand. The fact that our hands are so important makes it unsurprising that a great deal of information is stored in them. By studying the ancient art of hand analysis, and examining the outline of the hand, the fingers, and the skin patterns as well as the lines on the palm, the hand becomes a rich source of information. It can be an indicator of character and personality, a mirror of temperament and disposition, a register of our potential, and a record of the events that take place in our lives.

Dominant and Passive Hands

When assessing the hand, the question of right- and left-handedness, and which hand should be studied, is of fundamental importance. Practitioners of hand reading have long recognized that each hand registers and reveals different aspects of our lives. On right-handed individuals, the left, or passive hand, is associated with the private, intimate self, with imagination, instinctive reactions, natural aptitude, and potential abilities. This hand reveals information about childhood years, inherited tendencies, and congenital health. It represents the unconscious self. The right, or active, hand reveals the public persona of individuals and shows how they

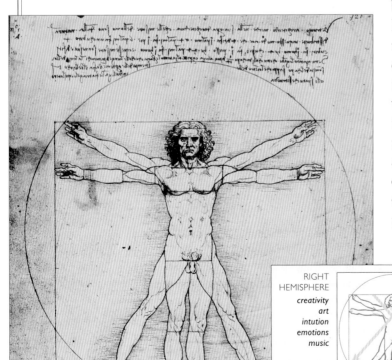

RIGHT HEMISPHERE		LEFT HEMISPHERE
creativity		logic
art		writing
intuition		speech
emotions		math
music		reading
OBJECTIVE		SUBJECTIVE

VITRUVIAN MAN
Leonardo da Vinci's depiction of a man drawn in proportions to fit both a square and a circle was inspired by the principles laid down by Marcus Vitruvius, the first-century BC Roman architect. Here, it serves to illustrate right- and left-handedness. For a right-handed person the left hemisphere of the brain controls the logical functions, and the right-hand side of the body. The opposite applies to those who are left-handed.

present themselves to the outside world. Details in this hand will relay information about your reasoning powers, show how talents are used, and how potential has been developed. This hand represents the conscious self, the mature adult. It also contains information about our health and the progress of events in our lives.

Left-handedness

Between 10 and 20 percent of the world's population is left-handed and of those, a slightly greater percentage are male. The scientific reason for right- and left-handedness was not understood until recently, but psychological and physiological studies have now confirmed what hand readers have believed for thousands of years. Their research has shown that the two hemispheres

of our brain control different functions. In right-handed people, the left side of the brain deals with the "logical" subjects such as reading, writing, calculation, and abstract thought, while the right side controls emotions, nonverbal communication, memory, and imaginative, intuitive, and creative processes. Commands from each hemisphere cross over and control the opposite side of our bodies, so that the left hemisphere sends messages to the right hand and vice versa. This, therefore, supports the belief of hand analysts that different elements of the character are contained in the two hands.

If you are left-handed, the roles are reversed. The right side of your brain rules the logical functions, and the left the emotional. Therefore, your left hand is your dominant hand and represents your conscious self; your right hand is your passive hand, and contains information about your childhood and potential.

THE FORTUNE-TELLER
Palmistry has been a recurring theme in art throughout the centuries. In 1594, Michelangelo Caravaggio (1573–1610) painted a gypsy reading the hand of a nobleman in La Buona Ventura *(The Fortune-Teller).*

THE HISTORY OF HAND READING

J UDGING BY THE NUMBER of hands painted on the walls of prehistoric caves, such as those of Wargata Mina in Tasmania, and Altamira in northern Spain, it would appear that the human hand has held a fascination for humans since the Stone Age. Archaeological discoveries have unearthed representations of hands carved out of stone, wood, and ivory as well as fashioned in metals by ancient civilizations across the globe. Etruscans even buried their dead with sculptures of hands beside the bodies in the graves. In fact, throughout history the hand has been studied, carved, and painted, has had curative and magical powers conferred upon it, has been used symbolically and in ritual, and has been worn as a talisman or token of luck.

Early Hand Reading

The existence of fingerprint patterns must have been recognized in China as far back as 3000 BC when the Emperor used his own thumbprint as a personal mark when sealing his documents. However, the earliest evidence that the hand, together with the markings in the palm, was used in the assessment of character and the prediction of future events, comes a millennium later. Sanskrit writings contain references to the "Samudrik Shastra," a system for interpreting the lucky marks and lines in the hand.

NOBLE HANDS
This woodcut depicts Barthélemy Coclès reading the hand of a nobleman. Coclès lived and worked in northern Italy in the 16th century and wrote several works on palmistry and other forms of divination.

GYPSY KNOWLEDGE
Gypsies were commonly associated with fortune-telling and palm reading. This print, after a painting by the Flemish artist David Teniers (1610–1690), depicts a gypsy reading the hand of a noblewoman, thought to be a portrait of the artist's wife.

Similar texts on the laws and practice of hand reading have also been found in Vedic scripts, while mention of the art is made in the Bible and in early Semitic writings. The geographical spread of hand reading suggests that it must have been in use among the ancient peoples of Sumeria, Chaldea, and Babylon, although no evidence is extant to date.

The Spread of Palmistry

The practice of hand reading, traditionally known as chirology, spread through Persia and Egypt to Turkey and Greece. Legend has it that, on one of his travels through Egypt, Aristotle (384–322 BC) discovered a treatise on the art of hand reading lying on an altar dedicated to the god Hermes.

The work, it is said, was in Arabic and written in letters of gold. Such was the impression the manuscript made upon him that Aristotle sent it to Alexander the Great (356–323 BC), extolling the benefits and value of the work and advising that it should be studied by all learned men. Recognizing its merits, Alexander promptly had the treatise translated into Latin, thus making the information available to European scholars, who were quick to take up the study. By the first millennium AD, hand reading had established itself throughout the world as an important branch of learning, valued by philosophers as a means by which to understand human dynamics, and by physicians as a diagnostic indicator of health.

Influential Practitioners

It was Aristotle who, through his own writings and observations on the functions of the hand, did much to disseminate the practice of hand reading. His work, *Chiromantia*, is one of the

EARLY DAYS
One of the earliest printed books was on the subject of hand reading, and was written by the Viennese, Johann Hartlieb, in 1448. The book, Die Kunst Ciromantia, was eventually printed in Augsburg in 1475, despite the fact that the practice of palmistry had been banned by the Christian church. Ironically, Hartlieb was a monk.

earliest surviving texts on the subject. The Roman orator Quintilian (AD 35–95) observed the role the hand plays in communication and may be regarded as one of the earliest exponents of nonverbal language. The Greek physicians Hippocrates (c. 460–c. 357 BC) and Galen (AD 130–200), considered the founders of modern medicine, were both knowledgeable about the use of the hand as a clinical aid. Galen made a special study of the thumb, and Hippocrates used the fingernails to aid diagnosis. Julius Caesar (102–44 BC), too, felt he understood enough of the principles of hand reading to enable him to judge his men by the shape of their hands.

The Decline

Despite its long line of distinguished and enlightened supporters, the practice of hand reading also had its share of detractors. Juvenal (AD 60–140), for example, made no secret of his animosity toward hand readers, whom he saw as charlatans and cheats. It was the Christian church, however, that was responsible for inflicting the greatest damage to the reputation of hand reading in Europe, perhaps in an attempt to stem the activities of unscrupulous practitioners who were preying on the vulnerable.

HANDS CARVED
Impressive colored wood-block illustrations from Chiromantiae, which was written in the first half of the 16th century by Barthélemy Coclès, the influential Italian chirologist.

The Christian church also considered palmistry to be rooted in paganism. In AD 315, a papal condemnation of palmistry and the threat of excommunication to anyone who participated in the art was to drive the practice of hand reading underground in Europe for the next thousand years. Elsewhere, and especially in the Arabic-speaking world, hand reading flourished and developed, particularly in the field of medicine.

The Renaissance

The Renaissance period, with its flowering of literature and art and its proliferation of ideas on nature and the universe, saw a renewed interest and acceptance of hand reading in Europe. The intelligentsia of the time, including many notable figures such as the orator Paracelsus (1493–1541) and later Robert Fludd (1574–1637), were to confer a new authority and respectability on the art of hand reading through their writings and personal observations.

Setbacks

However, while hand reading was enjoying a resurgence in mainland Europe, and even

BAD NEWS
Such was the rise in the popularity of palmistry during the late 19th century that Victorian cartoonists were quick to lampoon the practice. This cartoon by George du Maurier appeared in the magazine Punch *on February 12, 1887. It depicts two people who have been told they are incompatible as a couple.*

taught in universities in Germany, in Britain its progress suffered another setback as Parliament passed laws to ban its practice altogether. This time it was to be the growth of scientific curiosity through the 18th and 19th centuries, and in particular the Victorian desire to extend the boundaries of knowledge, that restored the reputation of hand reading. The art was also to be transformed quite radically and fundamentally by being treated as a science.

Science and the Hand

Many are the protagonists in the West who have contributed to the development of hand analysis and brought to it scientific validity. Two pioneers of skin ridge patterns were the 17th-century physician Nehemiah Grew, who lectured on his study of fingerprints in 1684, and Jan Purkinje,

FAMOUS HANDS
Count Louis Hamon, the world's most colorful and successful palmist, was born in Ireland and took his name Cheiro from the Greek word kheir, which means the hand. He lived in Britain and America at the turn of the last century and was consulted by many famous people, including statesmen and royalty.

THE PERSONAL TOUCH

Thumbprints have long been recognized for their uniqueness in China and have been discovered pressed into shards of ancient pottery as a form of signature. They provided the inspiration that was to lead to the use of fingerprinting in criminal identification.

published his thesis on fingerprint patterns in 1823. Stanislas D'Arpentigny (1798– 1865) and Adolph Desbarrolles (1801–1865) showed that hands can be classified according to their shape. Dr. Carl Carus, personal physician to the King of Saxony in the 19th century, matched hand types to personality characteristics. Dr. N. Vaschide, a French professor of pathology, published an essay on psychology and the hand in 1884. Advances in the fields of genetics, psychology, and forensics, especially since the late 19th century, have propelled the study of the hand into the modern age.

Fingerprints

The discovery of the uniqueness of skin ridge patterns and the cataloging of prints was to revolutionize police work worldwide when, in 1901, Scotland Yard adopted the technique of fingerprinting in criminal identification and investigation. Since then, medical researchers studying skin patterns, otherwise known as the science of dermatoglyphics, have discovered a correspondence between genetic abnormalities, such as Down's syndrome, and unusual markings in the hand. Continuing research in this field has recently confirmed a link between specific fingerprint patterns and heart disease.

Psychologists such as Hugo Debrunner, who made studies of hand types and gestures while he was a physician in the

Swiss Army during World War II, and Charlotte Wolff, who wrote many articles on the subject, including "The Human Hand" (1942) and "The Hands in Psychological Diagnosis" (1952), have observed and documented the relationship between the behavior we display and the gestures we perform with our hands and fingers.

East and West

Eastern hand reading remains an essentially intuitive art rooted in its origins and traditions, in marked contrast with the scientific emphasis that Western hand readers place upon their analyses. However, this by no means invalidates the Eastern practice and in fact there is much to be gained from the Asian approach. The art of hand reading is highly esteemed throughout the East where professional practitioners are consulted on a daily basis and on a wide variety of matters. Rather than condemning its use, both state and religion accept the practice as part of their cultural heritage and as an established branch of learning.

FINGER DANCER
Expressive gestures and hand movements are incorporated into the classical Eastern dances of the Thai and Kathakali performances, many of which have religious or mystical themes. Here, the Kathak, or professional storyteller, uses her hands to tell the story, each gesture carrying its own meaning and readily understood by the audience.

THE HAND IN COMMUNICATION

COMMUNICATION, WHICH is essentially the conveying of information from one person to another, is an acquired skill. We learn to communicate from the moment we are born; we learn to speak and to understand the spoken word, we mimic the behavior we see around us, and gauge the impact of our words and actions by the responses of others. We soon learn that communication is not just a matter of expressing our thoughts in words; we can also transmit messages without words, through the way we hold our bodies, alter our facial expressions, and make use of our hands.

Body Language

When we communicate with each other we listen to the conversation, and also pick up subtle clues from each other's gestures; this is known as nonverbal communication. We subconsciously give out information about ourselves and receive messages from those around us.

Although we use every part of our bodies to relay information about ourselves silently, our faces are perhaps the most expressive means of sending a wide range of signals, from love and happiness to anger and hate. Facial expressions – the manipulation of our mouth, eyes,

TRIUMPH
Raising the arms high into the air is one of the signals used in triumph. Here, F.W. de Klerk and Nelson Mandela raise their arms in a gesture that signifies political success. Their hands are joined as a symbol of the unification of the peoples in their nation.

eyebrows, even just the way we hold our head – are the easiest to control, but other parts of our bodies are less so, usually because we are not conscious of their movements. Actions involving the hands, for example, are just as numerous and revealing as facial expressions, but much more difficult to disguise. When there is a conflict or contradiction between what we are saying and the nonverbal cues that we are giving out, in the majority of cases it will be the body language that is responded to rather than the speech.

Gesture and the Hand

People who hold their hands close to their body tend toward introversion. They have quiet needs and may be fairly defensive types. In contrast, those who fling

HANDSHAKE
A handshake can signal dominance by placing the hand on top, palm down; submission by offering the hand palm up; and equality, as here between Mikhail Gorbachev and Ronald Reagan, with both hands in a vertical position conveying respect and a shared rapport.

POINTING
A fist with an extended index finger is a well-known guide signal, whether pointed at the self or showing direction. Jabbing the air while pointing at someone is a signal of aggression. Here, pointing directly at the onlooker, it becomes an authoritative command, bidding the viewer to pay attention and do as he or she is told.

BLESSING
Holding the index and middle fingers together and up-raised is a familiar pose of prelates in the act of giving a blessing, here performed by Pope John Paul II. The traditional Greek blessing is similar, but the thumb and ring fingers are crossed over the palm.

their hands out in wide, expansive gestures tend to be more extroverted, requiring a wider area of personal space to accommodate their outgoing personalities. There is a feeling of something secretive about palms that are hidden or hands that are stuffed into pockets, while hands held palm up are characteristically considered to signify openness and sincerity. Historically, open palms probably demonstrated that the individual could be trusted and that there were no weapons hidden in the hand. Outstretched arms have a variety of meanings according to how the hands are held. With palms held up facing an opponent, the message implies rejection or signals "keep off," or "keep your distance." If the palms are downturned, the signal is one of soothing the recipient. A single outstretched arm, with the hand cupped and held palm-side up is a well-known begging gesture, but if both arms are held out, it becomes a form of invitation or welcome.

THE SPARK OF LIFE
On the ceiling of the Sistine Chapel, Rome, Michelangelo has depicted God transmitting the spark of life through his index finger to Adam's inert hand. The gesture is reminiscent of a healer's touch restoring the health of the sick.

The Hand in Art

THROUGHOUT THE AGES, THE HAND HAS BEEN DEPICTED IN ART AS A SYMBOL.

———— • ————

SINCE ANCIENT TIMES hands have been used in cave paintings, drawings, sculpture, and fine art as symbols of communication. Particular finger positions or gestures of the hand, common to their age and civilization, delivered a message that was instantly recognized by those who understood the symbolism. Ancient Egyptian and Semitic art, for example, depicted celestial power by a hand painted in the sky. European religious painting represented the Holy Trinity by extending the thumb, index, and middle fingers of a hand. In fact, guides were written giving instruction to painters on how the hand was to be positioned in specific Christian attitudes, such as figures holding up their hands in a blessing pose. The index finger pointing upward has often been depicted as indicating the greater power of God in heaven.

SUPPLICATION
The traditional stance in prayer is the joining together of the two hands palm to palm. Sometimes the thumbs are crossed over each other, symbolically bending one's will to the greater good. However, when the joined-palms gesture is performed outside the religious context it becomes a signal of either persuasion or begging.

THE "V" SIGN
The "V" sign, in some situations a gesture of insult, has its roots in the war tactics of the Middle Ages. At the Battle of Agincourt in 1415, the French cut off the fingers of captured English archers in order to prevent them using a bow and arrow. The free English archers would wave their intact fingers at the French in a gesture of abuse and contempt.

The Role of Touch

Touching or holding someone by the arm or by the elbow is an acceptable social convention when guiding, steering, or attracting that person's attention. Touching or holding hands, however, is more personal and usually only occurs among people who are familiar with each other. The exception to this is the handshake.

Although essentially a gesture of greeting or of welcome, the handshake relays a wealth of information about each individual and the subsequent relationship they will have with each other. A limp

WAVING
A gesture of greeting or leaving, waving the hand takes several forms. In northern Europe it is common to wave the hand, palm showing, side to side. In Italy, however, the palm is turned around and the fingers are flapped up and down.

handshake suggests a weak, submissive personality. A forceful grip marks a dominant, aggressive type. Hostility and intimidation make themselves known by adding bone-crunching pressure to the grip. Interest and attraction is revealed by a handshake that is held for longer than is normal.

Finger and Thumb Gestures

Many gestures involve the fingers used either singly or in combination with each other. The index finger is the most flexible and versatile in nonverbal communication. It is the finger denoting the ego and it is therefore appropriate that it is used for pointing or calling attention to oneself or, when jabbing the air, to emphasize a statement, to threaten, admonish, show anger, or deride. Most rude or obscene gestures are made with the fingers, particularly the middle finger, for example, when it is sharply jerked into the air as a sexual insult. The ring finger does not figure prominently in gestures, possibly because it is unable to hold itself up straight without support from its neighbors. When the little finger is raised it is often associated with affection. The thumb, however, is the most important digit, as it represents willpower, determination, and control, and as such is used in a wide range of signals that vary around the world, from commands to confirmation, from insult to displays of superiority.

The Language of the Hand

THE HAND HAS ALWAYS BEEN USED IN COMMUNICATION, AND FOR SOME PEOPLE IT IS THE ONLY WAY THEY CAN MAKE THEMSELVES UNDERSTOOD.

THE USE OF HAND SIGNALS as part of nonverbal communication falls into three broad categories. The first entails the direct communication of meaning. Pressing an outstretched index finger to your lips, for example, communicates an order for silence. The second comprises the regulating mechanisms in a conversation or interaction. Here, body cues help the dialogue to flow – speeding it up, slowing it down or, with a raised hand, interrupting to give another participant the opportunity to take part in the conversation. The third category describes expression, or the management of one's feelings. Scratching your head to show perplexity is one such example, clapping your hand over your mouth to signal shock is another. A person may use these gestures subconsciously, and often the response to them is subconscious, too.

NATIVE AMERICANS
Sign language allows communication over a distance. Raising and lowering the index finger is a Native American signal of confirmation and acknowledgment.

SIGNING
In signing, the visual language of the deaf, it is the hand that talks. Words are communicated either through hand and arm gestures or spelled out by using the fingers to denote each letter of the alphabet. Here, the author's name is spelled in finger language.

L O R I

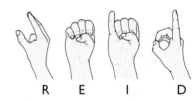

R E I D

Cultural Differences

When studying gesture and body language, it is most important to bear cultural differences in mind. Certain signals and gestures differ from nationality to nationality and from race to race. The classic hitchhiker's outstretched thumb, for example, may be recognized as requesting a lift in most parts of northern Europe, but there are certain parts of Greece where it would not be welcome as it is considered a personal insult. Very few, if any, signs are completely universal because they are often ancient products of different cultures.

VICTORY
Churchill's characteristic "V" for victory sign differs significantly from the insulting "V" gesture. When using this sign, the hand is held palm-side out and indicates there is nothing to hide. It is associated with success and triumph, and athletes often display this gesture after winning in competition.

WAGGING FINGER
Like shaking the head, wagging the index finger from side to side signifies "no." But wagging the whole hand with the index finger raised often accompanies a verbal admonishment, especially when performed by an adult and directed at a child.

THE ANATOMY OF THE HAND

G ALEN, THE GREEK PHYSICIAN, studied and described the functions of the hand in the first century AD. He noted its amazing ability to manipulate, grip, sense, and touch. In fact, the hand is the most versatile part of the human anatomy. The combination of 27 small bones and 37 skeletal muscles attached to the bones by tendons makes the hand an ingenious instrument capable of not only strong gripping action but also precise and delicate manipulation. However, it is the fact that we can bring together the tips of our thumbs and fingers, allowing a wide range of movement, plus the immense sensitivity of our fingertips, that makes our hands unique.

SENSE OF TOUCH

OUR SENSE OF touch is particularly acute in our hands because here, especially at the fingertips, our touch receptors, or sensory nerves, are highly concentrated. On average, we possess one hundred nerve endings per square centimeter on each fingertip, as opposed to five nerve endings per square centimeter on less sensitive parts of our bodies.

THE HAND BONES
The hand contains 27 bones. Of these, eight are found in the wrist or carpus, arranged into two interlocking rows to give articulation and to act as shock absorbers. From here, five metacarpal bones fan out through the palm and join the fourteen phalanxes that form the digits, three phalanxes per finger, and two for the thumb.

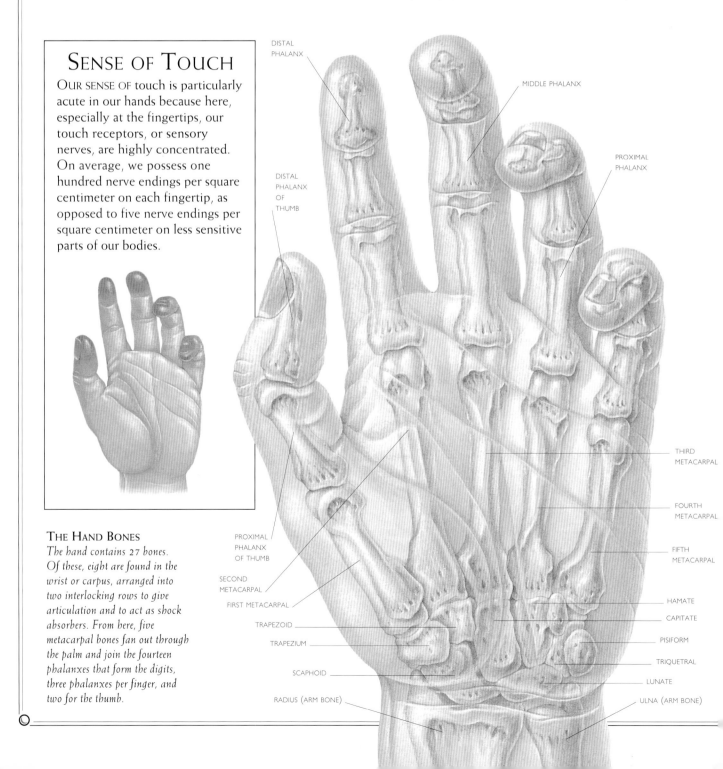

DISTAL PHALANX

MIDDLE PHALANX

PROXIMAL PHALANX

DISTAL PHALANX OF THUMB

PROXIMAL PHALANX OF THUMB

SECOND METACARPAL

FIRST METACARPAL

TRAPEZOID

TRAPEZIUM

SCAPHOID

RADIUS (ARM BONE)

THIRD METACARPAL

FOURTH METACARPAL

FIFTH METACARPAL

HAMATE

CAPITATE

PISIFORM

TRIQUETRAL

LUNATE

ULNA (ARM BONE)

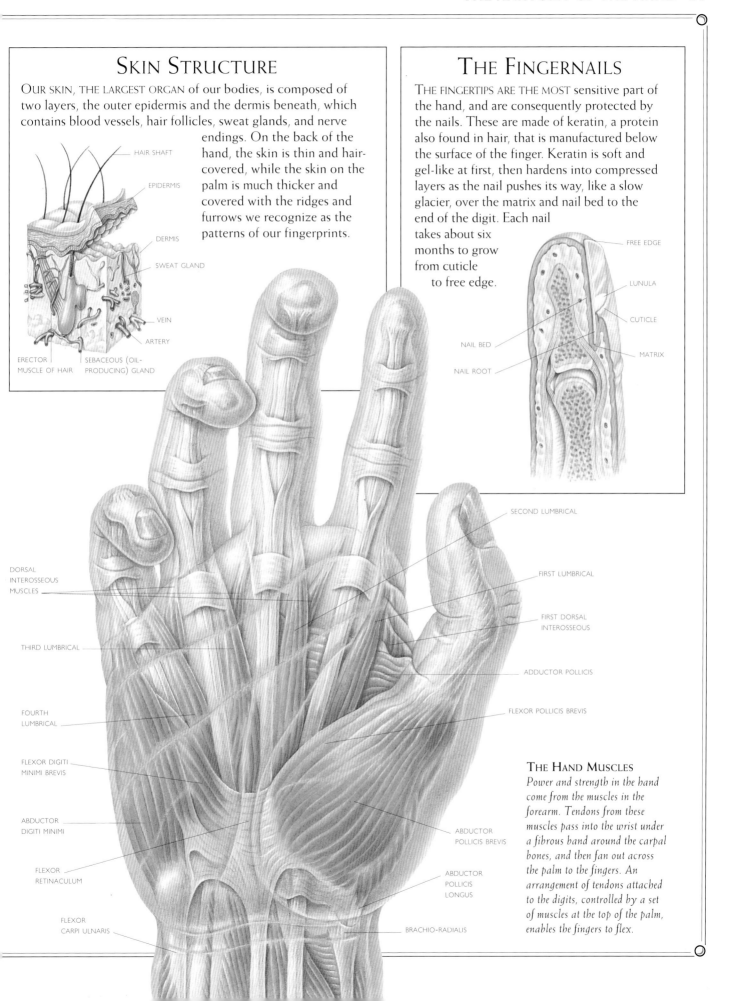

SKIN STRUCTURE

OUR SKIN, THE LARGEST ORGAN of our bodies, is composed of two layers, the outer epidermis and the dermis beneath, which contains blood vessels, hair follicles, sweat glands, and nerve endings. On the back of the hand, the skin is thin and hair-covered, while the skin on the palm is much thicker and covered with the ridges and furrows we recognize as the patterns of our fingerprints.

HAIR SHAFT

EPIDERMIS

DERMIS

SWEAT GLAND

VEIN

ARTERY

ERECTOR MUSCLE OF HAIR

SEBACEOUS (OIL-PRODUCING) GLAND

THE FINGERNAILS

THE FINGERTIPS ARE THE MOST sensitive part of the hand, and are consequently protected by the nails. These are made of keratin, a protein also found in hair, that is manufactured below the surface of the finger. Keratin is soft and gel-like at first, then hardens into compressed layers as the nail pushes its way, like a slow glacier, over the matrix and nail bed to the end of the digit. Each nail takes about six months to grow from cuticle to free edge.

FREE EDGE

LUNULA

CUTICLE

MATRIX

NAIL BED

NAIL ROOT

SECOND LUMBRICAL

FIRST LUMBRICAL

FIRST DORSAL INTEROSSEOUS

ADDUCTOR POLLICIS

FLEXOR POLLICIS BREVIS

DORSAL INTEROSSEOUS MUSCLES

THIRD LUMBRICAL

FOURTH LUMBRICAL

FLEXOR DIGITI MINIMI BREVIS

ABDUCTOR DIGITI MINIMI

FLEXOR RETINACULUM

FLEXOR CARPI ULNARIS

ABDUCTOR POLLICIS BREVIS

ABDUCTOR POLLICIS LONGUS

BRACHIO-RADIALIS

THE HAND MUSCLES

Power and strength in the hand come from the muscles in the forearm. Tendons from these muscles pass into the wrist under a fibrous band around the carpal bones, and then fan out across the palm to the fingers. An arrangement of tendons attached to the digits, controlled by a set of muscles at the top of the palm, enables the fingers to flex.

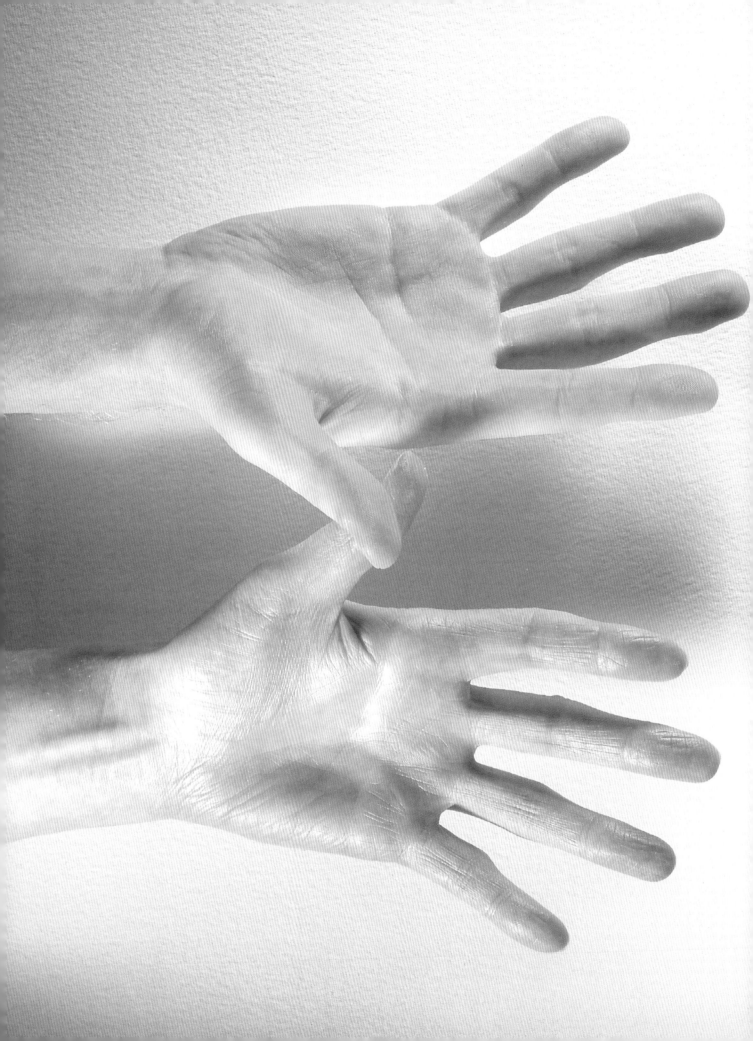

THE HAND

Hands come in many shapes and sizes, and no two are ever alike. Your hand is truly unique, and your very own personal signature.

READING THE HAND • THE SHAPE OF THE HAND
THE MOUNTS • OUTLINE FEATURES
THE FINGERS • FINGERTIPS AND PHALANXES
THE THUMB • THE FINGERNAILS • FINGERPRINTS
PALMAR RIDGE PATTERNS

READING THE HAND

FROM THE BASIC SHAPE of your hand to the smallest line in your palm, from the patterns on the tips of your fingers to the bands at the top of your wrist, every single feature in your hand contains valuable information about you. One of the best ways of accessing this information is through a study of your handprint. Handprints are invaluable for revealing the fine details that are hard to see or study on the living hand. They also, if taken at intervals, provide a record of the events that you experience throughout your life, and if taken of a child's hand will also record their growth.

HOW TO MAKE A HANDPRINT

TAKING HANDPRINTS can be messy and frustrating, particularly when areas of the hand fail to print or fingers move and smudge the ink. A little time and practice will help to perfect your technique and the results are worth it in the end. It does help to have the right equipment, but with a little ingenuity you will find alternatives around the house. A glossy magazine cover, for example, will substitute for the sheet of glass, and a rolling pin will work just as well as the printer's roller.

EQUIPMENT

- Water-soluble printing ink
- Sheet of glass or laminated plastic
- Table knife
- 4 in (10 cm) printer's roller
- Sharp pencil or felt-tip pen
- Sheets of paper

WATER-SOLUBLE PRINTING INK

FELT-TIP PEN

TABLE KNIFE

INK ROLLER

SHEETS OF PAPER

SHEET OF GLASS OR LAMINATED PLASTIC

1 Squeeze out a little of the ink onto the glass sheet. Use water-soluble printing ink because this will wash off with soap and water. Other inks may require special solvents.

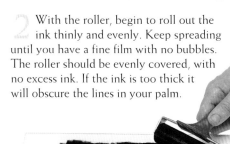

2 With the roller, begin to roll out the ink thinly and evenly. Keep spreading until you have a fine film with no bubbles. The roller should be evenly covered, with no excess ink. If the ink is too thick it will obscure the lines in your palm.

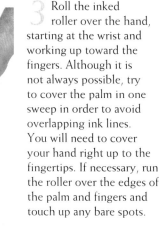

3 Roll the inked roller over the hand, starting at the wrist and working up toward the fingers. Although it is not always possible, try to cover the palm in one sweep in order to avoid overlapping ink lines. You will need to cover your hand right up to the fingertips. If necessary, run the roller over the edges of the palm and fingers and touch up any bare spots.

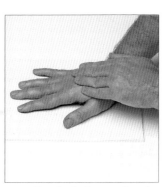

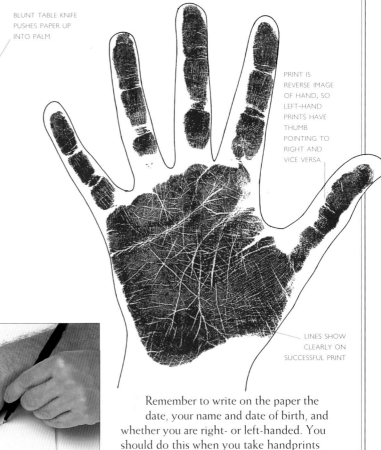

BLUNT TABLE KNIFE
PUSHES PAPER UP
INTO PALM

PRINT IS
REVERSE IMAGE
OF HAND, SO
LEFT-HAND
PRINTS HAVE
THUMB
POINTING TO
RIGHT AND
VICE VERSA

LINES SHOW
CLEARLY ON
SUCCESSFUL PRINT

Gently shake your hand in the air to loosen and relax the joints a little, then place it, in as comfortable a position as possible, on the paper and press down lightly.

Slip the table knife under the paper and slide it around the underside of your hand and wrist, pressing up into the contours and recesses of the palm. This should ensure that the lines in the hollow of the palm will show on the print.

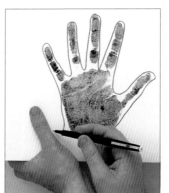

Now draw an outline around your hand. Keep as close to the hand as possible and take the line down to include 1–1¼ in (2–3 cm) of the wrist. If the print is not clear, try turning your hand palm upward, lay the paper on top, and press down.

Remember to write on the paper the date, your name and date of birth, and whether you are right- or left-handed. You should do this when you take handprints of your friends and family, too.

HOW TO MAKE A THUMBPRINT

IT IS IMPORTANT to be able to study the thumb for your analysis, but it rarely prints clearly enough when taking a print of the hand. Consequently, it is useful to make a special print of the thumb alone. As well as the thumbprint, the outline of the thumb is important when building a full personality profile (*see page 40*).

INK PAD   FELT-TIP PEN

EQUIPMENT
The same equipment used for taking the handprint may also be used here. An ink pad can make a good alternative but remember that the ink may require special cleansers.

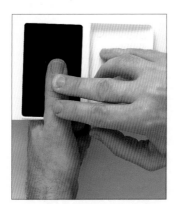

Either cover the thumb with a fine layer of ink using the roller, or, if you have an ink pad, press the thumb onto the pad, rolling it from side to side to cover the whole digit.

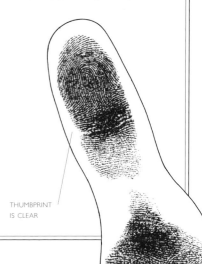

Whether printing only the thumb or adding it to the handprint, position the paper against the edge of the table so that the flat of the thumb and the web can be placed comfortably on the sheet.

Draw around the digit and note whether it is the right or left thumb. Ensure that the thumb is coupled with the corresponding handprint.

THUMBPRINT
IS CLEAR

THE SHAPE OF THE HAND

L EARNING TO IDENTIFY the shape of a hand, and deciding which category it belongs to, is one of the most important tasks in the art of hand reading. The shape of the hand determines the basic character of the individual, and constitutes the first building block of the personal profile.

All hands will conform to one of four categories, according to whether the palm is rectangular or square, and the fingers long or short. Each of these categories, classified as Earth, Air, Fire, and Water, describes a set of characteristics common to all members within the group.

THE EARTH HAND

HANDS BELONGING TO the Earth category have a square palm and short fingers. Known as the practical hand, it is associated with solid, sensible people who take a levelheaded, no-nonsense approach to life. Never afraid of hard work, owners of Earth-shaped hands are the first to roll up their sleeves and toil away at any task that confronts them. These people tend to be rather conventional and they have a great love of tradition. As friends and lovers they are thoroughly dependable and emotionally stable.

A PHOTOGRAPHER'S HAND
While the Earth hand describes someone who is practical, it is nevertheless often found on the hands of highly creative people. Artists and musicians, and those whose creative outlet requires them to possess great manual dexterity, are likely to have Earth-shaped hands.

THE EARTH HAND HAS
SQUARE PALM
AND SHORT FINGERS

THE FINGERS
The fingers belonging to the Earth hand are characteristically short, showing keen insight and inspirational talent, but also a tendency toward impatience.

THE LINES ON THE PALM
Typically, the lines on the palm of an Earth-shaped hand are few, but they are strongly marked and fairly deep. The head line, in particular, is often straight.

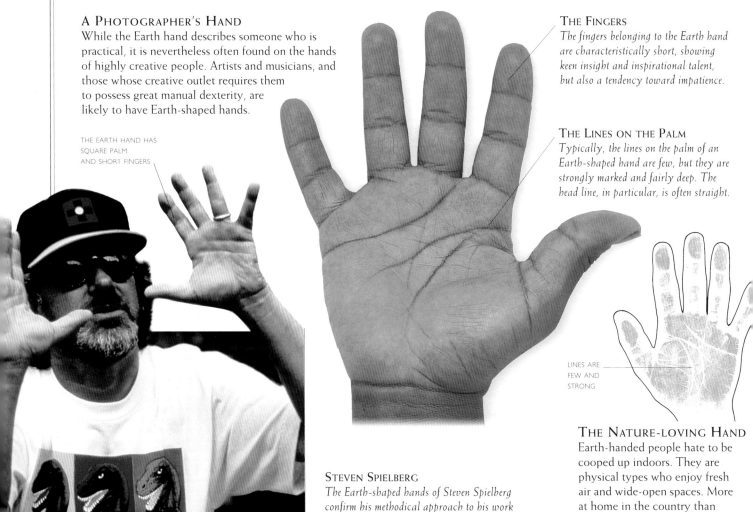

LINES ARE
FEW AND
STRONG

THE NATURE-LOVING HAND
Earth-handed people hate to be cooped up indoors. They are physical types who enjoy fresh air and wide-open spaces. More at home in the country than the city, they prefer to be close to the land, and enjoy a special rapport with nature.

STEVEN SPIELBERG
The Earth-shaped hands of Steven Spielberg confirm his methodical approach to his work and are a testament to his unflagging energies. It is these factors, combined with his inspired genius, that make him a master of his craft.

THE AIR HAND

THE AIR HAND, like the Earth hand, has a square palm, but the distinguishing feature here is the difference in the length of the digits, for this type has noticeably long fingers. Characteristically, people who belong to the Air group have a very active mentality. They are restless beings, possessing a sharp, inquisitive mind. A low boredom threshold, and a need for constant intellectual stimulation, mean that owners of the Air hand dislike repetitive, humdrum routine and have a constant craving for variety and change.

A WRITER'S HAND
Communication is the key to the Air person, and many belonging to this group display fine vocal or literary skills. Air-handed people excel at languages and often work in the media. The fields of writing, journalism, translation, and publishing are heavily populated by Air hands.

THE FINGERS
Although the palm of the Air hand is square, the long, supple fingers that are characteristic of this type lengthen the hand and give it an elegant appearance. The tips of the digits tend to be gently rounded or conic in shape.

THE LINES ON THE PALM
Typically, the Air palm has clear lines that are well defined. Though the lines are generally finer in appearance than those in the Earth hand, the palm as a whole has a firm and sturdy look.

PALM HAS FEW FINE, CLEAR LINES

THE MERCURIAL HAND
Gadgets and technological toys of every description delight those with Air hands. These people are likely to become computer whiz-kids, always familiar with the latest technology.

CLINT EASTWOOD
The controlled emotion of the Air category is manifested in the screen roles that Clint Eastwood has played. His foray into politics and public speaking is also typical of this type.

Embryonic Development of Lines

BABIES COME INTO THE WORLD WITH A FULL COMPLEMENT OF THE MAJOR LINES ALREADY FORMED AND STAMPED INTO THEIR HANDS.

THE MAIN LINES, heart line, head line, and life line, are formed in our hands around the third month of fetal development. Their construction is determined by our DNA blueprint. Congenital or chromosomal abnormalities, or any hiccup in the development process at this time, will affect the pattern and construction of the lines.

EVER-CHANGING LINES
Although the main lines in the hand are already formed at birth, they grow and change throughout our lives.

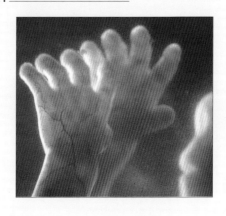

THE FIRE HAND

THE FIRE HAND is characterized by a long palm that is topped by comparatively short fingers. People who possess this hand shape tend to be vital and dynamic, with a lively, enthusiastic, happy-go-lucky nature. They cannot bear a quiet life and thrive on challenge and excitement, living their lives in the fast lane and burning the candle at both ends. Strong, positive, and charismatic, whatever they undertake is carried out with passion and zeal. People with Fire-shaped hands will naturally take the lead in any group.

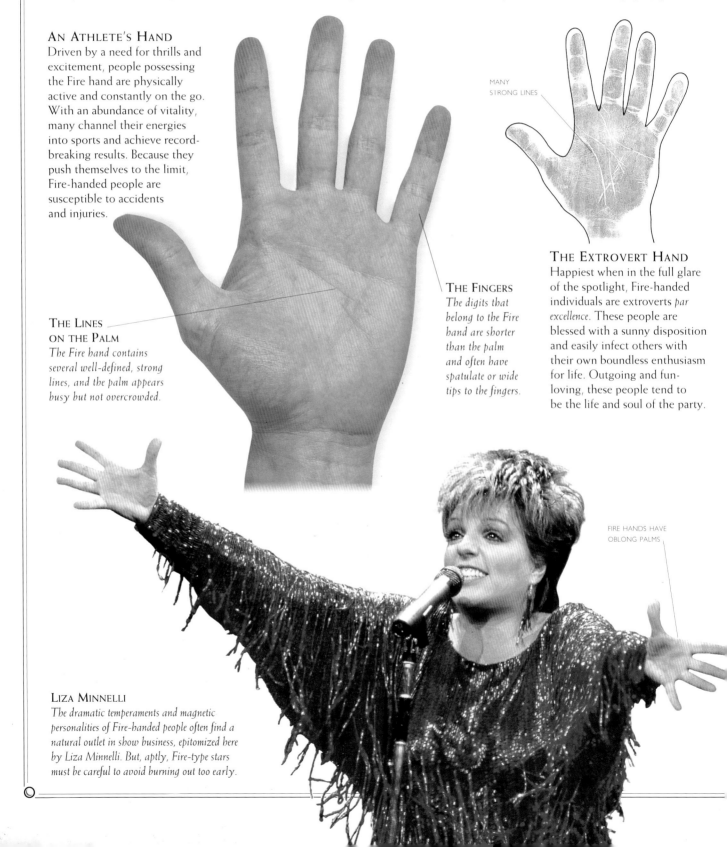

AN ATHLETE'S HAND
Driven by a need for thrills and excitement, people possessing the Fire hand are physically active and constantly on the go. With an abundance of vitality, many channel their energies into sports and achieve record-breaking results. Because they push themselves to the limit, Fire-handed people are susceptible to accidents and injuries.

MANY
STRONG LINES

THE FINGERS
The digits that belong to the Fire hand are shorter than the palm and often have spatulate or wide tips to the fingers.

THE LINES ON THE PALM
The Fire hand contains several well-defined, strong lines, and the palm appears busy but not overcrowded.

THE EXTROVERT HAND
Happiest when in the full glare of the spotlight, Fire-handed individuals are extroverts *par excellence*. These people are blessed with a sunny disposition and easily infect others with their own boundless enthusiasm for life. Outgoing and fun-loving, these people tend to be the life and soul of the party.

FIRE HANDS HAVE
OBLONG PALMS

LIZA MINNELLI
The dramatic temperaments and magnetic personalities of Fire-handed people often find a natural outlet in show business, epitomized here by Liza Minnelli. But, aptly, Fire-type stars must be careful to avoid burning out too early.

THE WATER HAND

LONG PALMS ACCOMPANIED by long fingers are the characteristics of the Water hand. Sensitivity is the hallmark of this group. Gentle and creatively gifted, these are the artists and poets, the musicians and visionaries among us. The world of the arts and the music industry are heavily populated with owners of the Water hand. People with this hand shape are often highly cultured and refined, with exquisite taste, but they are also unworldly, and have a tendency to live with their heads in the clouds.

THE FINGERS

The Water hand bears long, lean fingers, often with conic tips although they may sometimes be sharp and noticeably pointed. Long digits are a sign of patience and an eye for detail.

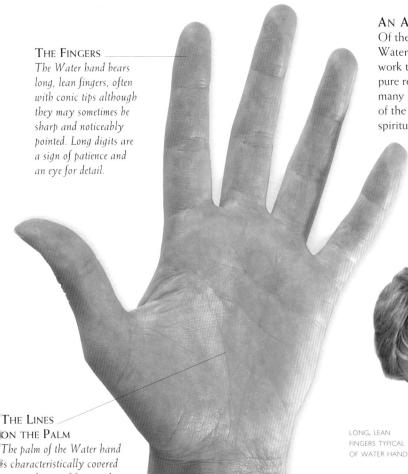

AN ASTROLOGER'S HAND

Of the four categories of hands, people belonging to the Water group are the least materialistic and they tend to work through intuition and emotion rather than through pure reason. Closely in tune with their own subconscious, many have psychic powers. Consequently, many owners of the Water hand interest themselves in psychological or spiritual subjects, whether of the orthodox or the complementary variety.

DIANA, PRINCESS OF WALES

The long, graceful appearance of the Water hand reflects elegance and style. People in this group are invariably chic and many are drawn to the beauty business or fashion industry, either as models or designers. Princess Diana's classic beauty and sophistication embody all the characteristics of the Water hand.

THE LINES ON THE PALM

The palm of the Water hand is characteristically covered in a profusion of fine, spidery lines – a testament to their owner's emotional nature.

LONG, LEAN FINGERS TYPICAL OF WATER HAND

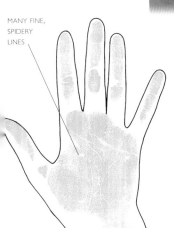

MANY FINE, SPIDERY LINES

THE SENSITIVE HAND

Vulnerable and often highly emotional, Water-handed individuals find it difficult to cope with the pressures of modern life. Ideally suited to a slower tempo, they dislike competitive situations and function best in a tranquil environment. Tractable and impressionable, they may lack independent judgment.

THE MOUNTS

O PEN AN ATLAS and usually you will see that each country is depicted in two ways. There is a physical geography map that charts features such as the mountains and flatlands. This is followed by a political map with the highways and railroads added. Now, open your hands. Your lines are like those highways and transportation routes, and they are embedded in a "land mass" whose terrain is contoured into a plain surrounded by the hills that are known as the mounts of the hand.

NAMING THE MOUNTS

THE PHYSICAL CONSTRUCTION of your palm is enough to reveal a wealth of information about you and your character. The palm is divided into nine padded mounts encircling a central plain. Each area has associations with a particular aspect of your personality. The characteristics of these aspects are epitomized by the classical name that has been given to each mount.

MOUNT OF JUPITER

Located around the root of the index finger, the mount of Jupiter represents your sense of authority and self-worth. If you are confident about yourself and your status in life this mount will be nicely rounded. Spreading over a wide expanse shows you are sociable and generous. Towering above the other mounts suggests burning ambition and bossiness.

MOUNT OF SATURN

Of all the mounts, this one is best if least developed, since too large a mount here denotes a gloomy disposition. Situated beneath the second finger, the mount of Saturn deals with your sense of responsibility. Overlarge reflects a solitary person who is cynical and ungiving. A slight padding reveals common sense and a love of philosophy.

MARS POSITIVE

Tucked into the crease of the thumb, Mars Positive represents courage, energy, and your fighting spirit and sense of self-preservation. When flat it denotes cowardice, but beware of aggression and cruelty with an overlarge development.

MOUNT OF VENUS

This mount provides the muscular padding under which is embedded the third bone of the thumb. Reflecting your enthusiasm for life, its development will directly reflect your stamina and vitality. Health, vigor, sex drive, and general joie de vivre are assessed by its shape and springiness. This area is usually more padded than the rest, but if exceptionally padded the libido is strong and the character unrefined. Overlean reveals delicate health. Well-rounded shows a warm heart and a sunny disposition.

MOUNT OF NEPTUNE

By its position, the mount of Neptune links the subconscious and the conscious sides of the palm and acts as a filter between them. Possessing a well-padded area here denotes quick perception and is seen in people with a charismatic personality. A deep valley reveals a lack of self-reflection.

THE DEVELOPMENT OF THE MOUNTS

EACH MOUNT REPRESENTS a store of energy that, by its shape and construction, suggests the strengths and weaknesses of the owner in the qualities associated with that mount. To see whether a mount is overlarge, well developed, or lean, you need to compare it to the other mounts in the hand. For instance, a lean hand will have relatively lean mounts, but one or two may be large or small in comparison with the rest.

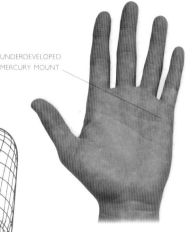

UNDERDEVELOPED
MERCURY MOUNT

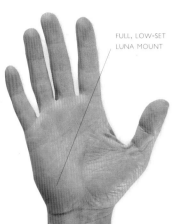

FULL, LOW-SET
LUNA MOUNT

AN UNDERDEVELOPED MOUNT
If a mount is poorly developed in comparison to its neighbors it reveals that energy or interest in the aspect represented by the mount is lacking in the individual's personality.

AN OVERDEVELOPED MOUNT
Apart from the mount of Venus, which is normally more developed than the rest, an inordinately dominant mount reveals that the characteristics associated with that mount are excessively prominent in the person's nature.

MOUNT OF APOLLO
Situated at the base of the ring finger, the mount of Apollo is associated with creative talent, artistic appreciation, and emotional vibrancy. People with a sunny outlook and a lively disposition invariably possess a rounded mount here. Poorly developed suggests a disinterest in the arts, while overdeveloped betrays ostentation and conceit.

MOUNT OF MERCURY
Found beneath the little finger, the mount of Mercury represents the ability to communicate with others. When well padded, the mount suggests a warm, receptive nature, while poorly developed tells of a lack of interest in other people. Overlarge is a sign of garrulousness.

PLAIN OF MARS
In the middle of the nine mounts lies the plain of Mars. This area reveals how well the passions and emotions are controlled. When thick and extensive it shows an irascible temper, but when lean and hollow the personality may lack impact or presence.

MARS NEGATIVE
Lying on the percussion (outside) edge between Mercury and Luna, Mars Negative depicts integrity, moral fortitude, and the courage of your convictions. Essentially, this area reveals staying power and the ability to cope under pressure.

MOUNT OF LUNA
The mount of Luna is associated with the imagination and subconscious, and represents sensitivity and intuition. It reveals the extent of our artistic talent and creative flair. Developed so that it overhangs the wrist tells of psychic leanings or a closeness to nature. Overlarge shows moodiness, while very lean reveals a poor imagination.

ASSESSING YOUR MOUNTS

IMAGINE A LANDSCAPE of rolling hills. Are the hills all of roughly the same size and height? Or does one dominate because it is much bigger or higher than the rest? Or, possibly, one hill is noticeably smaller, forming a dip on the horizon. Using this analogy will help when it comes to assessing your mounts, for it is crucial to determine how they stand in relation to each other. Gently cup your hand to make the mounts stand proud and look across your palm from wrist to fingers. Try to pick out which mount, if any, is dominant and which appears insignificant.

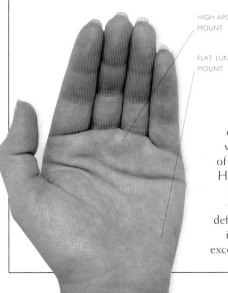

HIGH APOLLO
MOUNT

FLAT LUNA
MOUNT

CHANGING MOUNTS
Mounts that are exceptionally large will show an excess of energy or interest. However, if energies are rebalanced and interest redirected, deficient mounts will, in time, fill out and excessive ones reduce.

MARKINGS ON THE MOUNTS

MOST PEOPLE ARE AWARE of the major lines that cross the palm, for these are distinctive markings that we all possess in one form or another. Less conspicuous, and perhaps a greater source of curiosity, are the smaller marks that may be found scattered all over the palm. These markings are composed of tiny lines that form themselves into discreet patterns of five main types. They may not always be perfectly formed, but they should stand independently on the mount areas. Similar markings, found on the lines on the palm, have different interpretations, explained in *Introducing the Lines* on page 52.

IDENTIFYING THE MARKINGS

THE FIVE PRINCIPAL MARKINGS that are found on the mounts are the star, cross, grille, square, and triangle. Each signifies an influence on the qualities that the mount represents. In general, crosses and grilles are negative signs, symbolizing opposition or unfavorable energy directed toward the area of life represented by the mount. Stars announce good luck or financial gain, while triangles denote success accompanied by wisdom. Squares are a mark of protection and can soften the impact of a negative event.

STAR   CROSS   GRILLE   SQUARE   TRIANGLE

GRILLE ON MERCURY MOUNT
A grille indicates misdirected or scattered energy and here, on the Mercury mount, the mark implies unfocused or unstructured actions in business dealings.

STAR ON MERCURY MOUNT
Stars augur good fortune and success on most mounts. On Mercury, the mark denotes distinction in science or finance; on Apollo, prestige, especially in the arts; and on Jupiter, it heralds achievement and luck. On Saturn, however, it warns of difficulties in life.

CROSS ON MARS NEGATIVE
The cross is usually a negative sign symbolizing opposition or the attraction of unfavorable energies. Here, the marking denotes secret enemies or antagonistic forces.

GRILLE ON VENUS MOUNT
The grille represents a concentration of undirected energy and heightened tensions. On the Venus mount, it shows an extraordinary intensification of emotion.

STAR ON LUNA MOUNT
Traditionally, a star on the mount of Luna warns of dangers when traveling. The cross, too, carries a similar interpretation. If, however, the marking is enclosed in a square, the individual will be protected from harm.

TRIANGLE ON APOLLO MOUNT
Triangles suggest success, but with a rationalizing influence on the sphere of activity represented by the mount. With a triangle present, achievement is tempered with wisdom. On Apollo, therefore, fame and fortune would never go to the individual's head.

SQUARE ON SATURN MOUNT
On Saturn, most markings have a negative effect. The square, however, is a favorable mark, protecting the individual against personal or financial adversity.

CROSS ON JUPITER MOUNT
Another exception to the rule, a cross on Jupiter is not a negative sign. Rather, this is considered a symbol of a happy and fulfilling long-term relationship.

SQUARE ON JUPITER MOUNT
Although normally a sign of protection, on Jupiter the square has a unique meaning. Here, it is known as the Teacher's Square. Those possessing the mark are gifted instructors and teachers.

TRIANGLE ON MARS POSITIVE
Here, the triangle signifies the ability to channel constructively one's physical courage and strength. Military leaders and sportspeople with this mark can expect success in their careers.

CROSS ON PLAIN OF MARS
With so many major lines crossing this central plain of the palm, it is rare to find a freestanding mark. When a cross is found here it denotes an interest in complementary medicine or occult subjects.

THE DIVISIONS OF THE HAND

TAKE A LOOK AT HOW your hand is constructed. Is the base of the palm strong and thick, or is the top broader? Perhaps the percussion (outside) edge is more developed than the thumb side? Each area of the hand is associated with different aspects of our lives. By dividing the hand into zones and comparing the development of each section, we can ascertain which facets of our personality dominate and which we consider less important.

TWO ZONES

CONSCIOUS
The thumb side of your hand deals with your conscious awareness. Its development reflects the impact you make on the world at large.

SUBCONSCIOUS
The outside half of your hand represents your subconscious motivations and drives. Its construction reveals how much emphasis you place on the more intuitive, receptive, or spiritual side of your nature.

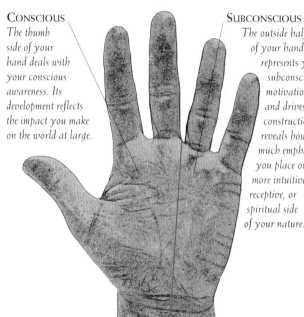

THREE ZONES

EMOTIONAL ZONE
The top zone of your hand is associated with aspirations and ideals. If this is the most highly developed area, it reveals that you approach life intellectually.

PRACTICAL ZONE
This area is the meeting ground of your physical and emotional energies. The strength of this zone reveals how you achieve a balance between the two.

PHYSICAL ZONE
The base of the hand reflects your primary drives and desires. Your basic needs as well as your physical energy are represented here.

FOUR ZONES

MENTAL, RATIONAL ZONE
In an ideal world, the four zones would be equally developed, to complement each other perfectly. In reality, a perfectly balanced hand is rare, and usually one area will be found to dominate the rest. When the mental/rational zone predominates, it reveals an ambitious personality. Underdeveloped suggests a lack of self-confidence.

MENTAL, INSTINCTIVE ZONE
When this zone predominates, the need to express oneself creatively is very important. Communication is of the essence, and this formation is often found in the hands of writers and artists, and scientists. Owners of a poorly developed zone here find different means of self-fulfillment other than through artistic creation.

PHYSICAL, PRACTICAL ZONE
Material considerations are prime motivators in the lives of those whose physical/practical zone predominates. When developed to excess, there is an abundance of energy that is channeled into activities that will bring physical gratification. When underdeveloped, though, vitality and enthusiasm may be absent.

PHYSICAL, INTUITIVE ZONE
This zone, comprising both the physical and subconscious elements of the personality, is associated with our intuition. Here is the area that represents our receptivity to the world around us. When this area predominates, the individual is spiritual and sensitive. Underdeveloped suggests its owner takes a very rational approach to life.

OUTLINE FEATURES

THE OUTLINE OF your hand will describe its construction – whether it is slender or broad, whether the fingers are smooth or knotted, whether the thumb joints are markedly angular, or whether the palm bulges at any point along the outside edge. These details provide remarkable insights into your personality, revealing information about your talents, how you think, and the direction in which you channel your energies. For this reason, drawing around the hand when taking a print is an essential part of hand analysis. Even without resorting to roller and ink, drawing a simple outline of the hand will help you to pick out these points of reference.

THE PERCUSSION

THE PERCUSSION is the area of the palm that lies on the outside edge of the hand. This area comprises the mounts of Luna, Mars Negative, and Mercury, and collectively these three areas represent our instinctive feelings and our creative potential. It is the shape of the percussion and the way it is formed that reveal how we bring the inner side of ourselves to life – in what guise we shape, channel, and express our inherent instincts and talents, and then direct them to the outside world. The fleshy percussion edge is prone to distortion when drawing around the hand, so it is important to exert only light pressure.

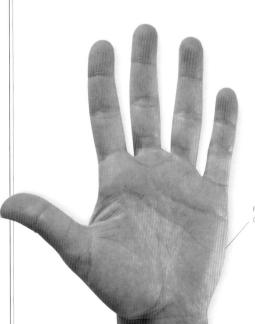

TAPERED PERCUSSION
A percussion edge that noticeably juts out beneath the little finger and then tapers down to the wrist emphasizes Mercurial energy. People with this formation have hyperactive minds and are mentally restless. Constantly planning, thinking, and turning ideas over in their head, they find it difficult to switch off and relax.

PERCUSSION CURVES OUT

PERCUSSION IS STRAIGHT

CURVED PERCUSSION
With a curved percussion, if the greatest development appears lower down near the wrist, creative talent is of a practical nature. Such people are better at interpreting the thoughts of others than in generating ideas of their own. A curve with a central bulge shows the ability to generate new concepts and the skills with which to put those ideas into practice.

PERCUSSION JUTS OUT

STRAIGHT PERCUSSION
Few percussions are truly straight for there is usually some slight padding. However, hands with flat percussions suggest that their owners have little interest in developing their creative faculties. They may also pay little attention to their unconscious minds. When a straight percussion exists, other parts of the hand will be developed, identifying the focus of interest.

ANGLES OF THE THUMB

WHEN THE JOINTS of the thumb are pronounced they form the angles of the thumb. A prominent top angle (*a*) is the sign of a stubborn person. If the second joint markedly juts out (*b*), it is known as the angle of manual dexterity. People whose hand forms a sharp angle where it joins the wrist (*c*), known as the angle of timing, have a love of music.

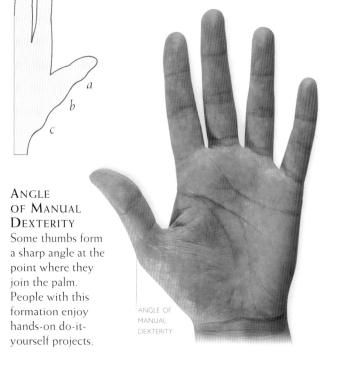

a
b
c

ANGLE OF MANUAL DEXTERITY
Some thumbs form a sharp angle at the point where they join the palm. People with this formation enjoy hands-on do-it-yourself projects.

ANGLE OF MANUAL DEXTERITY

THE KNUCKLES

FIST PRODUCES UNEVEN KNUCKLES

THE KNUCKLES ARE the joints between the bottom bones of the fingers and the bones that run through the palm to the wrist. When a fist is made, some hands form a smooth, corrugated line of joints while others are knobbly and uneven. Smooth knuckles belong to those who are meticulous about their appearance and fastidious about their living environment. Uneven knuckles suggest a more relaxed approach to life.

FINGER JOINTS

ARE YOUR FINGERS SMOOTH OR KNOTTY? With smooth fingers the outline is straight, but with knotty fingers the silhouette is decidedly bumpy. There are two types of knotty fingers. Those with pronounced top and bottom joints are known as

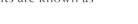

FINGERS ARE SMOOTH

philosophical fingers. The second type has large joints only in the bottom, or basal, set where they are known as knots of material order. Establishing the difference is important as this will reveal how you process information and express your thoughts.

KNOTS AT TOP AND BOTTOM JOINTS

SMOOTH JOINTS
People with smooth-sided fingers are receptive to external stimuli and information. Ideas and impressions are taken in and processed intuitively. Smooth fingers, therefore, are a mark of impulsive action and thought.

PRONOUNCED JOINTS
With philosophical fingers, thinking is methodical and information is analyzed with care before it is acted upon. When only the basal joints are pronounced, the individual is a careful thinker and needs to live in orderly surroundings.

THE FINGERS

THROUGH OUR FINGERS we give expression to our talents, each finger representing a different sphere of interest. Do any of your fingers stand out? If one is longer, straighter, or less developed than the rest, it may reveal something about your personality. Length should be assessed first. If your middle finger is almost as long as your palm, you have long fingers: less than three-quarters of the length of your palm means your fingers are short. Long fingers denote a love of detail, while short-fingered people are quick on the uptake, and perceive the whole at a glance.

NAMING THE FINGERS

EACH FINGER REPRESENTS a different area of life, and is traditionally named after one of the mythological beings – Jupiter, Saturn, Apollo, and Mercury – whose characteristics express that digit's area of influence. The size and shape of each finger shows the extent to which you possess the qualities it represents.

JUPITER – THE INDEX FINGER
In classical mythology, Jupiter was the chief god and ruler of the world. Traditionally, the index finger is named after him, because it represents ego, leadership qualities, and one's position or standing in the world. Your assertiveness and ambition are shown here. A straight index finger denotes integrity, a very long index finger shows bossiness, while a short index finger tells of timidity and self-doubt.

SATURN – THE MIDDLE FINGER
The middle finger is named after Saturn, the father of Jupiter, and is associated with wisdom. This finger reveals how you deal with responsibility, and whether you have a serious or careless attitude to life. A long middle finger suggests an industrious mind but also that humor may be lacking. If the middle finger is short, it denotes an irresponsible personality.

APOLLO – THE RING FINGER
Apollo was the sun god, and is traditionally associated with music and poetry. Your ring finger reflects your creativity and sense of well-being. A strong ring finger is often seen on the hands of entertainers and artists. A weak ring finger suggests a lack of creative talent, while a very long ring finger may reveal a gambling instinct.

MERCURY – THE LITTLE FINGER
Mercury, the messenger of the gods, is associated with communication. This finger reveals your powers of self-expression, and the longer it is, the more articulate you are likely to be. A short Mercury finger suggests you may have difficulty in putting your thoughts into words. Traditionally, a curved little finger indicates shrewdness, but can also denote untrustworthiness and deceit.

FINGER SPACING

WITH YOUR hands resting comfortably on a table or on your lap, observe how the fingers are placed in relation to one another. If all of the fingers are bunched tightly together, you are a gregarious person, who feels much happier in company than alone. If all the fingers are wide apart, it shows openness and is a sign of the extrovert. The spacing between the fingers can also be significant.

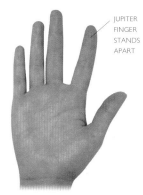

JUPITER FINGER STANDS APART

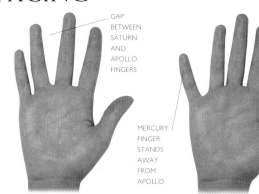

GAP BETWEEN SATURN AND APOLLO FINGERS

MERCURY FINGER STANDS AWAY FROM APOLLO

JUPITER STANDING APART
Intellectual independence and ambition are characteristics found in people with a Jupiter finger that stands away from the rest. These people like to make up their own mind.

MIDDLE FINGERS APART
If these fingers are held apart, it suggests a resourceful, independent nature. People with this spacing need some time by themselves each day for their peace of mind.

MERCURY STANDING APART
A wide gap between the Apollo and Mercury fingers shows independence. People with this formation do not like to feel hemmed in, either physically or psychologically.

FINGER SETTINGS

STRENGTH OF CHARACTER and other personality traits may be deduced from the way the fingers are set into the palm. Look at the line formed where your fingers meet your palm. Is it straight, curved, or uneven?

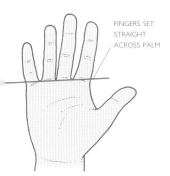

FINGERS SET STRAIGHT ACROSS PALM

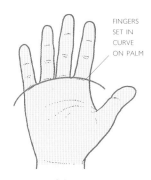

FINGERS SET IN CURVE ON PALM

STRAIGHT SETTING
Evenly set fingers are fairly uncommon but when found they denote confidence and assurance. Endowed with good sense and a positive attitude, these people cannot fail to become successful in life.

ARCHED SETTING
An arched setting suggests a nature that is neither arrogant nor timid. It indicates a person with a well-balanced personality.

UNEVEN SETTING
When the Mercury finger sits much lower than the other digits, it reveals a marked lack of self-confidence. When the Jupiter finger is noticeably lower set, watch out for an inferiority complex in the individual.

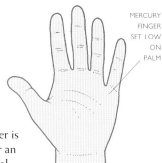

MERCURY FINGER SET LOW ON PALM

Polydactyly and Anne Boleyn

ABOUT 50 BABIES IN EVERY 100,000 ARE BORN WITH EXTRA FINGERS OR TOES.

THESE DAYS POLYDACTYLY, as possession of extra digits is known, is a recognized genetic anomaly that runs in families. The extra digits are usually surgically removed after birth. During the Middle Ages, however, a sixth finger became associated with sorcery, and its owner was thought to be versed in witchcraft and the black arts. Rumor has it that Anne Boleyn, wife of Henry VIII and mother of Elizabeth I, had six fingers on each hand. Reputedly, she always wore her sleeves long in an attempt to conceal her "witches' hands." Indeed, her enemies even referred to her as "Anne the witch."

ANNE BOLEYN
Ancient superstition associated extra fingers with good luck. Not so for Anne Boleyn, who was beheaded in 1536 by order of Henry VIII.

FINGERTIPS AND PHALANXES

THE SHAPE OF THE fingertips reveals how an individual's interests are expressed to the outside world. Much of this information can be gleaned from the sections of the fingers known as phalanxes, a term also used to describe the bones inside the fingers. Every finger is made up of three phalanxes, and each phalanx should be assessed for any unusual development, such as excessive length, thickness, or thinness, that causes it to stand out in some way from its companions. The top, middle, and bottom phalanxes represent different spheres of interest, and any marked discrepancy highlights an accentuation or relative absence of interest. By evaluating the formation of each individual phalanx, you can identify and give precise definition to the more general qualities that are associated with the fingers to which they belong.

FINGERTIP SHAPES

VERY FEW HANDS POSSESS fingers that all end with tips of the same shape. More often than not, several different shapes will be found on one hand. Under these circumstances, each fingertip must be analyzed in turn, bearing in mind, first, the quality that is represented by the finger and, second, how that quality will be expressed through the particular shape of its tip. As a quick reminder, the Jupiter finger is associated with the ego, the Saturn finger represents our sense of responsibility, the Apollo finger deals with art and creativity, and the Mercury finger deals with communication.

SQUARE FINGERTIPS
People with square fingertips are careful and methodical thinkers. The square shape, being the mark of a practical character, is found in the hands of those who take a rational view of life. What their owners lack in creativity, they more than make up for in skilled know-how.

POINTED FINGERTIPS
Pointed tips to the fingers denote a sensitive and fragile personality. Artistic talent and strong imaginative powers are much in evidence, but owners of these fingers tend to be daydreamers and prone to flights of fancy. They are associated with writers, poets, and theoreticians.

CONIC FINGERTIPS
Conic fingertips symbolize a creative turn of mind. Possessing this type of finger reveals an appreciation of the arts and a flexible disposition. People with conic fingertips are happy to flow with the prevailing circumstances, but emotional security is important for their peace of mind.

SPATULATE FINGERTIPS
The spatulate shape is associated with action and people possessing this type of fingertip tend to be dynamic thinkers and have an original mind. They have advanced ideas and are mentally ahead of their time. The shape is associated with inventors, explorers, and pioneers.

THE MEANING OF DROPLETS
PEOPLE POSSESSING DROPLETS – little rounded pads that resemble drops of water seemingly about to drip off the tops of the fingers – have a tactile nature. Also referred to as sensitivity pads, they reveal an acutely developed sense of touch. They may not appear on all the fingers but even one or two will show a love of texture.

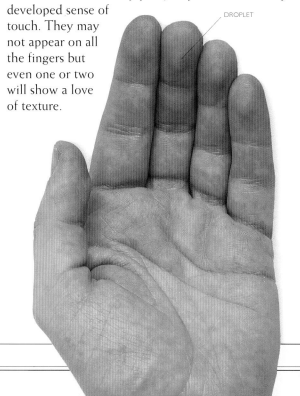

DROPLET

THE PHALANXES

THE SHAPE AND DEVELOPMENT of the top phalanxes of the fingers reveal how we react intellectually to the characteristics represented by each digit. How we apply our talents in those areas is highlighted by the formation of the middle phalanxes. The basal phalanxes describe our physical or instinctive reactions.

JUPITER

TOP PHALANX
Look out for a highly materialistic character when this section is short, and doubly so if it is also thick. A long phalanx is a sign of perspicacity.

MIDDLE PHALANX
Superefficiency is revealed by a long section here and excellent managers possess this formation. Short reveals a lack of ambition.

BOTTOM PHALANX
A short section here denotes a laid-back attitude. Long tells of a bossy nature. Thin denotes fastidiousness but also a connoisseur.

SATURN

TOP PHALANX
Seriousness and a love of research are both denoted by a long top section. Shorter adds a steadying influence. A skeptical attitude is revealed by a thin top phalanx here.

MIDDLE PHALANX
A very short section denotes a scientific mind. A long section shows an efficient manager. A thick section indicates a "green thumb."

BOTTOM PHALANX
Here, a long basal phalanx implies self-centeredness, while a short one suggests a penny-pinching nature.

APOLLO

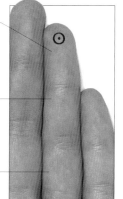

TOP PHALANX
A long top phalanx reveals an intellectual appreciation of art, but overlong brings out narcissistic tendencies. A spatulate tip highlights dramatic qualities.

MIDDLE PHALANX
Long and lean shows artistic flair with a good eye for line and color. Short or thin symbolizes poor artistic judgment.

BOTTOM PHALANX
A very long basal section here denotes acquisitiveness. Short tells of poor taste, while padded reveals a hoarder or collector.

MERCURY

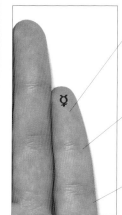

TOP PHALANX
Excellent powers of articulateness accompany a long top phalanx here, and if the tip is pointed it reveals persuasiveness. A short phalanx implies a lazy mind.

MIDDLE PHALANX
Financial flair is associated with a long middle section. Short suggests a disorganized mind. Thick denotes unscrupulousness.

BOTTOM PHALANX
Naïveté belongs to those with a short basal section. A long one reveals self-delusion. Thick suggests a lack of imagination.

PHALANX FEATURES

ALTHOUGH IN PRINCIPLE each phalanx stands on its own merit and must be assessed individually, sometimes sets of phalanxes may be evaluated as a group. Long middle phalanxes and full basal ones are particularly worthy of note.

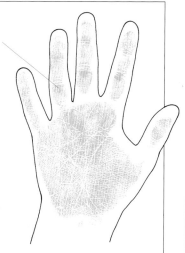

LONG MIDDLE PHALANXES

FULL BASAL PHALANXES

LONG MIDDLE PHALANXES
A hand with noticeably long middle phalanxes belongs to a cautious, thrifty individual. These people manage their affairs, at home and at work, with precision and efficiency.

FULL BASAL PHALANXES
A set of basal phalanxes that are full and round denotes a certain sensuality in one's nature. Self-indulgence and a penchant for the good life may be much in evidence.

THE THUMB

A FEAT OF ENGINEERING, the thumb is a technological wonder. Set in opposition to the fingers, its action enables us to grip and manipulate objects with amazing dexterity. Its development on our hands gives us the ability to create, to turn dreams into reality and, in doing so, shape our universe and control our environment.

No wonder, then, that the thumb is believed to represent willpower and strength of character. It is a measure of force and drive, essentially revealing how much initiative we possess. What is more, its formation pinpoints how that initiative is used and applied – whether logically or intuitively, subtly or aggressively, intermittently or sustained.

CHARACTERISTICS OF THE THUMB

LIKE THE FINGERS, the thumb is composed of three sections. The top and middle phalanxes constitute what we recognize as the thumb proper. But the basal section is embedded in the hand and forms part of the mount of Venus. Your thumb can be assessed as a whole and you can also analyze each phalanx in turn.

UPPER PHALANX
The top phalanx of your thumb represents your willpower, determination, and tenacity of purpose. Depending on its length, shape of the tip, and general formation, it reveals your driving force – how much energy you are prepared to put into whatever you undertake.

LOWER PHALANX
How you apply your driving force is determined by the development of the lower phalanx. Its shape and construction are a measure of your intelligence and powers of reasoning. It reveals how logical you are in your actions.

THUMB SHAPES

THE SHAPE OF THE THUMB describes how will and logic are blended in the individual's personality. The tip then reveals how these are expressed externally. A square tip, for example, will give the thumb a blunt appearance, symbolically revealing a lack of subtlety in dealing with others. A shapely thumb reveals greater mental agility and excellent powers of perception.

POINTED
The more pointed the thumb, the more impulsive the owner. Such individuals possess a sensitive nature but are adept at manipulating other people's feelings.

SPATULATE
Driven by adventure and excitement, owners of the spatulate thumb have an original mind. Do not confuse this shape with the bulbous thumbtip (*see page 41*).

SQUARE
Practical, logical, and law-abiding, owners of square thumbs play by the rules. Level-headedness is their trademark, and honesty and fairness their approach.

CONIC
Eloquence and a creative turn of mind are signified by this shape. Appearances are important and the owner likes to make a good impression on others.

PHALANX THICKNESS

FURTHER VALUABLE CLUES about your character and personality may be gleaned from the thickness of your thumb, both by assessing the digit as a whole, and by looking at the phalanxes individually. Essentially, the thickness of the thumb describes the manner in which you come across to other people – subtle or brusque, pushy or persuasive, self-motivated or relaxed.

Before evaluating the phalanxes, the thumb itself must be judged against the rest of the hand. The two should appear harmoniously balanced. If the thumb looks very large in relation to the palm, the individual may be overly dominating and aggressive. If the thumb appears small, weak, or thin, the individual lacks dynamism.

UPPER PHALANX

THIN TIP

TIP IS THICK AND FLESHY

LOWER PHALANX

TIP IS THICKER THAN LOWER PHALANX

THICK LOWER PHALANX

THIN TIP
From the side, this phalanx appears to be shaved off up to the tip. Owners of this thumb are adept at social interaction because they have keen psychological insight.

BULBOUS TIP
A thick thumb with a bulbous tip accompanies a pushy and aggressive nature. Sometimes called a clubbed thumb, its owners have a tendency to be obstinate and unreasonable.

THIN LOWER PHALANX
Thin phalanxes imply subtlety, and when the middle section is pinched in, it is known as a "waisted" thumb. The feature marks a pleasant disposition and reveals tact and diplomacy.

THICK LOWER PHALANX
Owners of this thumb type often lack tact and may be considered insensitive and imprudent by others.

PHALANX LENGTH

THE TOP PHALANX OF the thumb represents your willpower, while the second symbolizes your powers of reasoning. Therefore, for the best effect, the two phalanxes of the thumb should be of equal length.

If this is the case, determination is tempered by rational thought, and plans are able to be brought to fruition through willpower. In reality, it is far more common to have one phalanx longer than the other.

SHORT TOP, LONG BOTTOM
This combination produces lots of plans and good intentions, but enthusiasm tends to peter out before the ideas are brought to fruition. It is very much a case of the spirit being willing but the flesh weak.

LONG TOP, SHORT BOTTOM
A long top phalanx is the mark of a doer but the short second section reveals a lack of reflection. Owners of this pairing often fail to question their motives, or to evaluate a task critically.

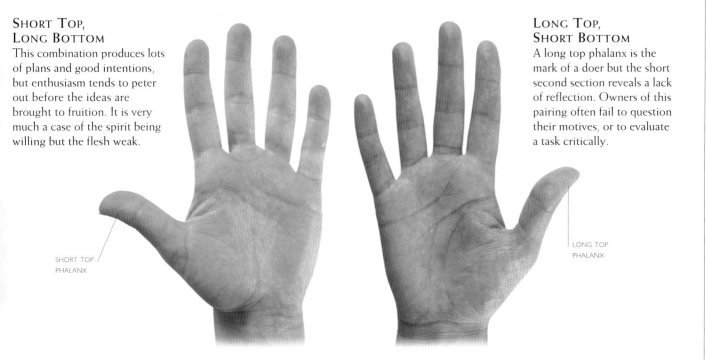

SHORT TOP PHALANX

LONG TOP PHALANX

THE POSITION OF THE THUMB

IF CHARACTER AND TALENTS are to be coordinated and successful, the thumb must be in proportion to the rest of the hand. A thumb needs to be measured against the hand to establish its relative strength or weakness. One that appears markedly to dominate the hand is considered strong – the more the thumb overshadows the palm and fingers, the stronger it will be. A thumb that looks insubstantial in relation to the rest of the hand would be deemed weak. Strong thumbs bring results, even in a hand with few talents marked. Weak thumbs let potential talents go to waste. The way in which your thumb is set into your hand can tell you whether you are a natural extrovert or introvert, and how closely you hold your thumb against your palm reveals how you relate to other people.

Thumb Gestures

FROM THUMB-SUCKING TO THE THUMBS-UP SIGNAL, THUMB GESTURES ARE USED IN BODY LANGUAGE ALL OVER THE WORLD.

———— • ————

FORMING A CIRCLE by joining together the tips of the thumb and forefinger is, in some, but not all nationalities, a recognized signal implying that a matter is okay, or, better still, perfect. The thumbs-up gesture has a similar meaning. Derogatory signals involving the thumb include the "get lost" message performed by jerking the thumb sharply over one's shoulder.

CROSSED THUMBS
Clasping the hands so that the fingers are interlaced and the thumbs crossed is a gesture of reassurance, but making a steeple of the fingers and thumbs signals self-confidence.

THUMB SETTINGS

WHETHER THE THUMB takes root high up on the hand or lower down distinguishes those who are mentally inspired from those who take their inspiration from practical activities. With a low setting, the thumb often appears to stand out and away from the palm, forming a wide angle, while with a high setting, the thumb is more likely to be positioned close to the palm, creating a narrow angle of opening.

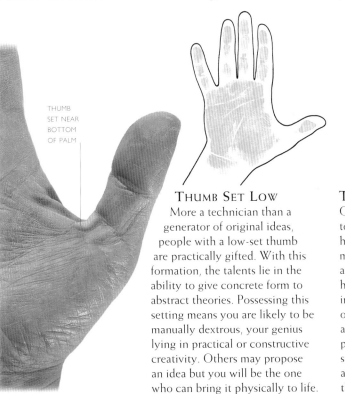

THUMB SET NEAR BOTTOM OF PALM

THUMB SET LOW
More a technician than a generator of original ideas, people with a low-set thumb are practically gifted. With this formation, the talents lie in the ability to give concrete form to abstract theories. Possessing this setting means you are likely to be manually dextrous, your genius lying in practical or constructive creativity. Others may propose an idea but you will be the one who can bring it physically to life.

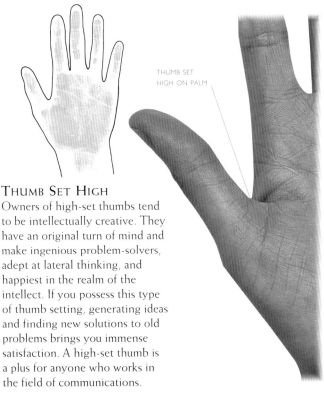

THUMB SET HIGH ON PALM

THUMB SET HIGH
Owners of high-set thumbs tend to be intellectually creative. They have an original turn of mind and make ingenious problem-solvers, adept at lateral thinking, and happiest in the realm of the intellect. If you possess this type of thumb setting, generating ideas and finding new solutions to old problems brings you immense satisfaction. A high-set thumb is a plus for anyone who works in the field of communications.

ANGLES OF OPENING

YOUR MOODS AND YOUR ATTITUDES toward others are reflected by the angle your thumb forms when it opens away from the palm. If the angle is tight, the hand will appear more closed and the personality will be more guarded. A wider angle suggests a more expressive, friendly, and outgoing nature.

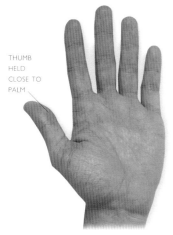

THUMB HELD CLOSE TO PALM

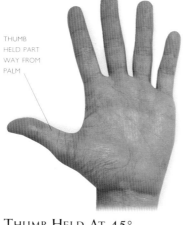

THUMB HELD PART WAY FROM PALM

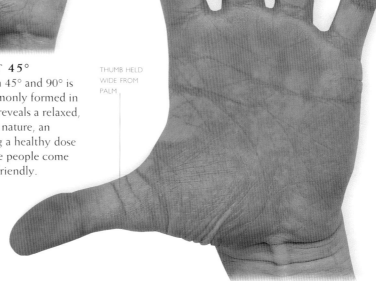

THUMB HELD WIDE FROM PALM

THUMB HELD CLOSE

Thumbs that form a narrow angle to the palm denote an inhibited nature and a cautious, reserved personality. While determination and persistence are marked, this formation may reveal narrow-mindedness. Selfishness is also present if the hand is pale and lean.

THUMB HELD AT 45°

Opening to between 45° and 90° is the angle most commonly formed in the normal hand. It reveals a relaxed, open, and confident nature, an individual possessing a healthy dose of self-esteem. These people come across as warm and friendly.

THUMB HELD AT 90°

Asian hand readers maintain that a thumb that opens to 90° denotes a well-balanced individual. However, when the angle is greater than 90°, the nature becomes too expansive, extroversion is marked, and its owner lacks self-control. Lack of concentration means that energies are not channeled.

THUMB FLEXIBILITY

FLEXIBILITY OF THE THUMB is calculated by the "give" in the top joint. If the top phalanx feels as if it is fused to the second section so that the tip of the thumb refuses to bend, the digit is considered stiff. If the top phalanx bends backward at the joint in a gentle curve the thumb is judged to be flexible.

THUMB IS RIGID AND INFLEXIBLE

A STIFF THUMB

A stiff thumb is the mark of fixed attitudes and an unyielding nature. People with this formation are both resistant and persistent. They have strong powers of concentration and, with a will of iron, can focus on a task until they reach their objective. Obstinate, determined, and very often opinionated, people with stiff thumbs are reserved, but forceful in nature.

A FLEXIBLE THUMB

A flexible thumb symbolizes an adaptable, accommodating individual, someone who is happy to go along with the flow. It is unusual to find the owner of this thumb swimming against the tide. Intellectually open and creatively oriented, they are prepared to consider diverse ideas, and often take on far too much responsibility. Easily contented, they also tend to be easily distracted.

THUMB BENDS EASILY BACKWARD

THE FINGERNAILS

Our fingernails reveal considerably more about us than many people realize. Badly bitten nails, for example, are associated with a nervous or anxious disposition. Brown stains on the Jupiter and Saturn fingers reveal that the individual is a smoker. Beautifully manicured tells of personal pride, while nails that are ungroomed belong to someone with less fastidious habits. But our nails can disclose much more information than merely giving telltale clues about our behavior and lifestyle. The shape, construction, and color of our nails can describe our character and temperament. The nails also register the impact of any major event that occurs in our lives and, because of their constant rate of growth, act as a timing gauge, recording when the incident took place. Even more importantly, our nails are a useful source of information about our state of health and well-being – a factor that was recognized as long ago as 400 B.C. by Hippocrates, who believed that the nails reflect the condition of the inner body.

CHARACTERISTICS OF THE FINGERNAILS

NAILS COME IN A VARIETY of shapes and sizes. Ideally, they should be smooth and lustrous, with a springy texture and, depending on race, an even pink or beige color, accompanied by a milky white moon. When assessing the shape and size of your nails, only the "quick," or colored part is taken into account. Because it is no longer living, the white tip should not be included in the evaluation of the fingernail.

NAIL SHAPES

SQUARE
Indicative of an easy-going nature and even temperament. The larger the nail, the more well-balanced the individual. If the nail is small it denotes a cynical point of view.

BROAD
Rectangular nails that are broader than they are long are mostly found only on the thumb. These reveal a strong character with a volcanic temper that quickly blows itself out.

FAN-SHAPED
Also referred to as shell-shaped, the fan-shaped nail is associated with a nervous disposition. Nails may occasionally adopt this shape when their owner has been under long-term stress.

ALMOND
Owners of the almond-shaped nail are gentle, kind people. Often creative, they possess a dreamy disposition. They may lack physical and psychological robustness.

NARROW
Most nails are narrow on the little finger, but a whole set of narrow, talonlike nails denotes a cold nature. The individual has a tendency to be selfish and self-centered.

NAIL GROWTH PATTERNS

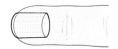

VERTICAL RIDGES
Vertical ridging in the fabric of the nails produces a ribbed texture. When present, these show a tendency toward skin or rheumatic conditions.

HORIZONTAL RIDGES
Horizontal ridging may be attributed to dietary deficiencies. Single grooves point to particular events, such as a crash diet, illness, or shock.

DISHED
Dished nails are invariably a sign of chemical imbalances due to nutritional deficiencies that, if uncorrected, may lead to serious illness.

WRAPAROUND
A nail that hooks over the fingertip suggests a grasping nature. Physically, however, this denotes a tendency toward respiratory problems.

THE MOONS

PRODUCTION OF THE NAIL takes place below the surface of the finger, behind the cuticle. The semicircular lunula, or moon, at the base of the nail is part of the dense-growing root and shows through the layers as milky white. Even in hands where few moons are visible, they are more than likely to be found on the thumbs. Overlarge moons suggest a predisposition to an overactive thyroid gland, while no moons at all may suggest an underactive one. In general, a weaker constitution is associated with moonless nails. Poorly formed moons may point to a predisposition to heart disease, and moons that are tinged with blue denote respiratory disorders and possible cardiovascular problems.

MOON

MOON CHARACTERISTICS
The size, shape, and color of the moons are inherited and will therefore reveal any familial predisposition to poor health and disease.

FINGERNAIL COLOR

IDEALLY, THE COLOR of the fingernails should be even and of a lighter hue than the prevailing skin tone on the back of the hand. In the European hand, the nail bed shows a pinkish color through the keratinous layer, while that of the African hand appears a creamy beige. Yellow, brown, or blue discoloration gives diagnostic clues about the health of the individual. Spots, blotches, or blemishes of color, such as white specks, are often indicative of nutritional imbalance.

RED FINGERNAILS
Physiologically, redness in the nails points to a predisposition to poor circulation. A red pigmentation of the nail bed is also associated with a choleric disposition. Red nails denote an irascible temper with angry, impatient moods.

PALE FINGERNAILS
Nails that appear significantly paler than the surrounding skin on the back of the fingers may point to an iron deficiency. As for character, a very pale, white, or grayish tinge to the nails is often a sign of selfish tendencies.

The World's Longest Nails

HISTORICALLY, VERY LONG FINGERNAILS WERE ASSOCIATED WITH WEALTH AND STATUS. THEY SIGNIFIED THAT THEIR OWNER DID NOT DO MANUAL WORK.

HAVING GROWN HIS FINGERNAILS for over 40 years, India's Shridhar Chillal has entered the record books as the proud possessor of the longest recorded nails in the world. His shortest nail is on the left index finger and measures a mere 40 in (102 cm), considerably shorter than the one on his thumb which is 52 in (132 cm). Shridhar, who was born in 1937, last cut his nails in 1952. There are many folklore traditions attached to the cutting of nails. According to certain customs, the best days of the week on which to trim one's nails are Mondays and Tuesdays. Wednesdays and Thursdays are also considered favorable, while Friday brings bad luck. To cut one's nails on a Saturday, it is said, is destined to attract losses, and those who trim their nails on Sunday will suffer some great misfortune before the week is out!

RECORD-BREAKER
Shridhar Chillal displays the longest recorded nails in the world.

FINGERPRINTS

P ATTERNS IN THE SKIN were first documented in 1823 by Dr. Jan Purkinje, a Czechoslovakian physician. He noticed that the skin covering the palm side of the hands had a surface of ridges and furrows that form into patterns. Each fingerprint pattern is unique, to the extent that the patterns on the right hand do not exactly match those on the left. Unlike the lines in the palm, while the fingerprint patterns grow in size from child to adult, they never change. Cut, burn, tear, or abrade away the skin, with the healing process the pattern returns exactly the same as before.

FINGERPRINT PATTERNS

PRINTS ARE CLASSIFIED INTO three main pattern types – the loop, whorl, and arch, which are subdivided to include variations. Each pattern type is associated with particular characteristics, giving clues about your personality. Count the patterns on your fingers. The prevailing type reveals your predominant strengths.

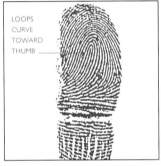

LOOPS CURVE TOWARD THUMB

ULNA LOOPS
The most common pattern, ulna loops sweep in from the direction of the percussion and point toward the thumb. They reveal an adaptable, easygoing attitude, with a need for many interests and activities.

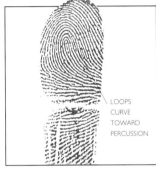

LOOPS CURVE TOWARD PERCUSSION

RADIAL LOOPS
A fairly unusual type of loop, these sweep in from the direction of the thumb and point toward the percussion. As flexible and amenable as people with ulna loops, their owner is more self-assertive.

COMPLETE CIRCLES

CONCENTRIC WHORLS
A complete set of whorls is rare and the pattern is more usually found on the thumb, Jupiter, or Apollo fingers. This pattern shows an inflexible but responsible character who prefers to be in charge.

SPIRAL

SPIRAL WHORLS
Although less intense than the concentric version, spiral whorls suggest similar traits, such as fixed attitudes and strongly held views. Owners of this pattern are happiest working alone.

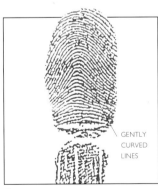

GENTLY CURVED LINES

ARCHES
Rarely found on the Mercury finger, arches belong to people with practical abilities. Solid, hardworking, and reserved, they see life from a materialistic point of view.

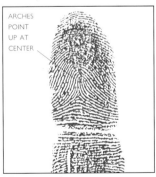

ARCHES POINT UP AT CENTER

TENTED ARCHES
An unusual pattern, so-called because of the "tentpole" at the center of the arches. Owners share qualities of the simple arches but are more enthusiastic and impulsive.

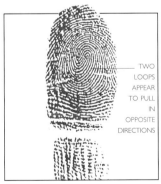

TWO LOOPS APPEAR TO PULL IN OPPOSITE DIRECTIONS

COMPOSITES
Formed in the shape of two loops pulling in opposite directions, this reveals open-mindedness, an ability to see a problem from all perspectives, but also indecisiveness.

WHORL INSIDE A LOOP

PEACOCK'S EYE
A tiny whorl enclosed in a loop, this rare pattern is usually found only on the Apollo or Mercury fingers. It is a sign of luck or preservation, conferring protection upon its owner.

PATTERN CHARACTERISTICS

THE TYPE OF PATTERNS YOU POSSESS and their positions on your fingertips will reveal your approach to life. Some people have the same fingerprint pattern on every finger. More usually, people have a mixture of patterns. It is important to analyze a pattern in the context of the finger on which it appears.

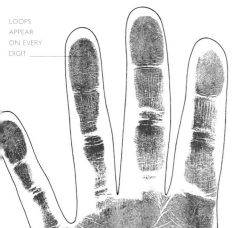

LOOPS APPEAR ON EVERY DIGIT

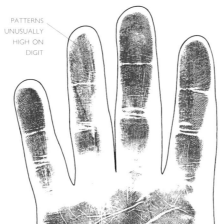

PATTERNS UNUSUALLY HIGH ON DIGIT

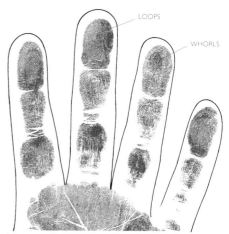

LOOPS

WHORLS

COMPLETE SET OF ONE PATTERN

The same print occurring on all 10 digits accentuates the qualities represented by that pattern. For example, a complete set of loops emphasizes flexibility, while practicality is pronounced with arches.

PATTERN SETTING

Normally, the core of a pattern is located approximately at the center of the top phalanx, but if it appears high up the focus of the energy is intellectual. If low down, the energy is used in practical ways.

MIXED PATTERNS

Assess each pattern according to the digit's influence. On the thumb, personal drive; Jupiter finger, ambition; Saturn finger, security; Apollo finger, fulfillment; and the Mercury finger, communication.

LEAVING PRINTS

OUR SKIN RIDGES are punctured by rows of tiny pores through which we perspire. When we touch an object, we deposit tiny beads of perspiration which have been emitted from each pore, subsequently leaving an impression of our ridge pattern behind.

TELLTALE SIGNS

The fingerprints we leave on objects are known as latents. Even the driest hands will leave impressions behind.

Fingerprints and the Police

BOTH THE US AND GREAT BRITAIN USE THE GALTON METHOD OF FINGERPRINTING DEVELOPED IN THE LATE 19TH CENTURY. THIS METHOD OF PERSONAL IDENTIFICATION REVOLUTIONIZED POLICE WORK WORLDWIDE.

ON SEPTEMBER 13, 1902, one Henry Jackson was sentenced to seven years for his part in a burglary. It was the first time a jury had passed a verdict of guilty on the evidence of a thumbprint spotted by a policeman at the scene of the crime. The technology in the identification of criminals has made huge advances since that first historic occasion. Yet, even with today's developments in electronic storage techniques, laser detection equipment, and computerized retrieval facilities, hours of manpower are still required to detect, lift, and match latents to stored fingerprints in police files.

POLICE FILES

The onset of technology has revolutionized police fingerprint records. Computers were first used to store fingerprints in the 1970s. At last count, the FBI computer had more than 70 million fingerprints stored in its files. The computer at New Scotland Yard in London contained almost five million fingerprints.

PALMAR RIDGE PATTERNS

THOUGH MOST OF US are aware of the skin prints on our fingertips, we may not realize that we possess similar patterns on our palms. In fact, the whole of our palmar surface is covered by skin which, among its many unique properties, contains ridges and furrows that flow, sometimes in parallel lines, sometimes in the familiar patterns of loops and whorls that we find on our fingertips. These patterns are genetically inherited and are stamped into our hands around the third month of fetal development. They are useful for highlighting special qualities in our nature.

TYPES OF RIDGE PATTERNS

LOOPS ARE THE MOST COMMON pattern on the palm, whorls appearing far less frequently. Some hands contain several patterns, while others have none. The most usual location for patterns is high up on the palm, dropping from the webbing between the finger bases. Alternatively, they may be found on the mounts of Venus and Luna (*see page 49*). Hands with no patterns have what is called an "open field" print.

RIDGES AND FURROWS
The study of the skin markings on the hand is known as dermatoglyphics. The term, deriving from the Greek words *derma* meaning skin, and *glyph*, which means a carving, describes the rows of ridges and furrows that appear to be carved into the skin.

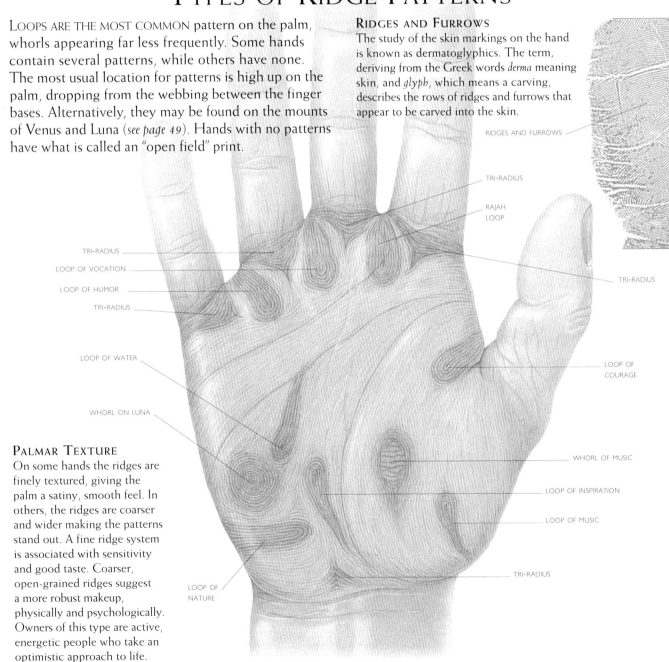

RIDGES AND FURROWS

TRI-RADIUS

RAJAH LOOP

TRI-RADIUS

TRI-RADIUS

LOOP OF VOCATION

LOOP OF HUMOR

TRI-RADIUS

LOOP OF WATER

WHORL ON LUNA

LOOP OF COURAGE

WHORL OF MUSIC

LOOP OF INSPIRATION

LOOP OF MUSIC

TRI-RADIUS

LOOP OF NATURE

PALMAR TEXTURE
On some hands the ridges are finely textured, giving the palm a satiny, smooth feel. In others, the ridges are coarser and wider making the patterns stand out. A fine ridge system is associated with sensitivity and good taste. Coarser, open-grained ridges suggest a more robust makeup, physically and psychologically. Owners of this type are active, energetic people who take an optimistic approach to life.

TRI-RADII

WHEN SEVERAL RIDGES FLOW TOGETHER and meet, they form a triangular pattern known as a tri-radius. Tri-radii are said to be focal points of energy.

FINDING THE TRI-RADII
We possess several tri-radii in our hands, but usually the most easily visible are those that lie at the top of the palm around the base of each finger.

LOOPS

THOUGH THEY MAY OCCUR elsewhere in the palm, the most frequent location for the loop is starting on the webbing between the fingers, or on the top mounts.

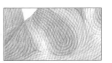

LOOP OF HUMOR
Found between the Apollo and Mercury fingers, this pattern denotes a dry sense of humor and a cheerful disposition.

LOOP OF VOCATION
Found between the Apollo and Saturn fingers; when present this pattern reveals dedication to work and career.

THE RAJAH LOOP
A rare marking located between the Jupiter and Saturn fingers, it highlights leadership qualities and is said to indicate noble blood.

LOOP OF COURAGE
Another unusual pattern, this loop enters the palm above the thumb joint. Its presence reveals a courageous spirit.

LOOP OF MUSIC
A loop that sweeps in from the thumb edge and rises up onto the mount of Venus is associated with an appreciation of music.

LOOP OF INSPIRATION
Rising up the center of the palm from the wrist, this loop, denoting inspirational creativity, is associated with poets and artists.

LOOP OF NATURE
A loop across the mount of Luna implies a rapport with living things. Owners of the mark are sensitive and attuned with nature.

LOOP OF WATER
Flowing down toward the Luna mount, this pattern tells of an affinity for water. Being near water is therapeutic for its owner.

WHORLS

WHORLS ARE SELDOM FOUND between the fingers and are rare in the palm, but occasionally one may appear on the Venus mount and another on the Luna mount.

WHORL OF MUSIC
A very rare find, the whorl enclosing a patch of horizontal ridges on the Venus mount is called a "bee" because it resembles the insect. It denotes strong musical talent.

WHORL ON LUNA
The whorl is a pattern of intensity that, when located on this mount, reveals a concentration of imaginative talent – a boon for actors, painters, and writers.

The Rajah Loop

ACCORDING TO INDIAN TRADITION, THE RAJAH LOOP IS THE MARK OF ROYAL BLOOD.

MARY QUEEN OF SCOTS
Mary Stuart was Queen of Scotland from 1542 to 1567.

ASIAN HAND READERS maintain that anyone who possesses a loop between their Jupiter and Saturn fingers must be descended from royalty. Consequently, they have conferred the title of Rajah to this extremely rare marking. In the West, however, hand readers are reluctant to make such grand associations, although it is recognized that those who possess the loop often achieve positions of power and high status in their lives. Interestingly, though, it has been observed that some people who possess the mark, but no evidence of nobility, strongly suspect that they have noble blood in their ancestry.

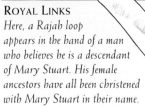

ROYAL LINKS
Here, a Rajah loop appears in the hand of a man who believes he is a descendant of Mary Stuart. His female ancestors have all been christened with Mary Stuart in their name.

THE LINES

The lines in our hands act as registers, recording events and suggesting the possible outcomes of our actions and decisions. However, our lines can and do change according to the conscious choices we make, providing a chart of our progress and development throughout our lives.

INTRODUCING THE LINES • THE LIFE LINE
THE HEAD LINE • THE HEART LINE
THE FATE LINE • DISCREPANCIES BETWEEN
HANDS • THE APOLLO LINE
SECONDARY LINES AND PATTERNS

INTRODUCING THE LINES

People with no knowledge of hand analysis sometimes suggest that the lines in our palms are nothing more than creases caused by bending our hands and fingers. If this were the case, why, one might ask, do we not all have identical markings? Why are some people's hands covered by a great many lines while others' possess only the bare minimum? And why do people who work with their hands frequently have far fewer lines in their palms than those in clerical or managerial professions? Our lines are not simple creases, created by repeated movements. They are created by our nervous system and linked to our physiology and body chemistry.

THE MAJOR LINES

The life line, head line, and heart line are formed during the first few months of fetal development and, just as we inherit the color of our hair, the strength and direction of our lines, as well as the shape of our hands, are also genetically determined.

   The other major lines are usually formed later on. Sometimes a baby may have a complete set of lines at birth, but usually they appear gradually, as the child matures. Our lines do not remain static but change and evolve in response to our own progress and development through life.

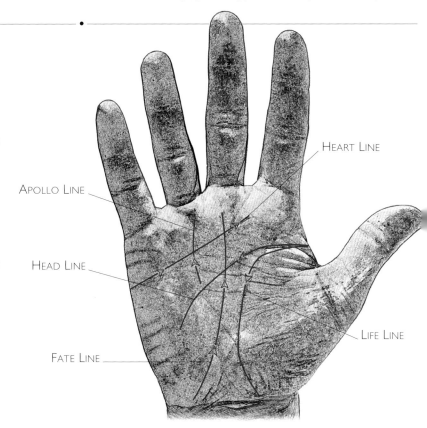

HEART LINE

APOLLO LINE

HEAD LINE

LIFE LINE

FATE LINE

LINES OF DESTINY
The china model, above, shows the major lines. The arrows indicate the direction in which they should be read.

MARKINGS ON THE LINES

If you think of your hand as a map, and the lines as roads, imagine that your lines carry messages from your body chemistry. Lines that are strong and well formed suggest that your path is clear, but markings on the lines are like obstructions on a road, and warn of obstacles and events in your life. A break in a line suggests a change of direction, while crosses and bars symbolize opposition. Stars represent a time of intensification of energies. Islands weaken the line and indicate periods when resistance is low. A sequence of islands, known as a chain, further weakens the line. Branches are like side roads, leading to another area of the hand. A square formation affords protection through times of difficulty.

| OVERLAPPED BREAK | CLEAN BREAK | BAR | STAR | ISLAND | BRANCH | CROSS |

THE SECONDARY LINES AND MARKINGS

IF THE MAJOR LINES are compared to truck routes and highways, the secondary lines and markings are the minor roads. Just as minor roads conduct traffic to a final destination point, so the secondary markings add the final flourishes to a character analysis, acting as beacons that point out refinements of the personality.

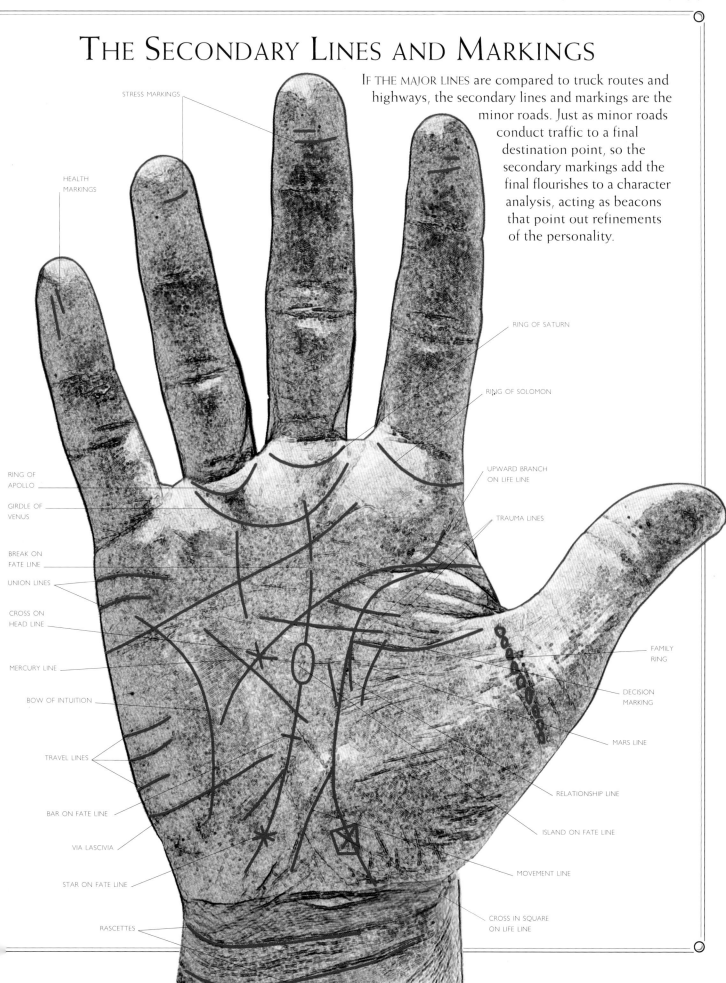

STRESS MARKINGS

HEALTH MARKINGS

RING OF APOLLO

GIRDLE OF VENUS

BREAK ON FATE LINE

UNION LINES

CROSS ON HEAD LINE

MERCURY LINE

BOW OF INTUITION

TRAVEL LINES

BAR ON FATE LINE

VIA LASCIVIA

STAR ON FATE LINE

RASCETTES

RING OF SATURN

RING OF SOLOMON

UPWARD BRANCH ON LIFE LINE

TRAUMA LINES

FAMILY RING

DECISION MARKING

MARS LINE

RELATIONSHIP LINE

ISLAND ON FATE LINE

MOVEMENT LINE

CROSS IN SQUARE ON LIFE LINE

THE LIFE LINE

CONTRARY TO POPULAR BELIEF, the life line is not an indicator of longevity. Short life lines have been found in the hands of people who have lived to their nineties, while long ones have been recorded in the palms of individuals who have died at a relatively young age.

What the life line does reveal, however, is the quality of your life, not the length, for this line acts as a clear and unequivocal record of your physical and psychological state of health. It is a visible gauge that measures, according to its construction and the path it takes around the ball

of the thumb, your vitality, your level of energy, and your physical strength. In the life line you can see if you have been blessed with a robust constitution or if your stamina is below par. Your life line will reflect whether you are physically active, courageous, and outgoing, or nervous, timid, and inward-looking. Also reflected in the construction of this line is your enthusiasm and zest for living.

Whether you will remain indomitable and cheerful in the face of adversity or whether you are likely to buckle at the first sign of pressure will be directly mirrored in this line.

CHARACTERISTICS OF THE LIFE LINE

BEGINNING AT THE EDGE OF THE PALM, between the thumb and Jupiter finger, the life line sweeps its way down and around the mount of Venus toward the

wrist. Some life lines form a shallow arc, tightly skirting the ball of the thumb. Others flow out in a curve that sweeps toward the center of the palm.

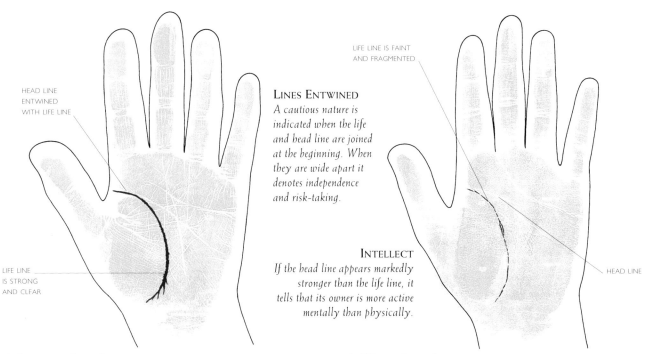

HEAD LINE ENTWINED WITH LIFE LINE

LIFE LINE IS STRONG AND CLEAR

LINES ENTWINED
A cautious nature is indicated when the life and head line are joined at the beginning. When they are wide apart it denotes independence and risk-taking.

INTELLECT
If the head line appears markedly stronger than the life line, it tells that its owner is more active mentally than physically.

LIFE LINE IS FAINT AND FRAGMENTED

HEAD LINE

A STRONG LIFE LINE
The stronger the life line, the more robust and vigorous is the constitution. If you have a well-etched line you are tough and resilient, and you will cope with whatever life brings. With plenty of energy at your disposal you may excel at sports. If the life line appears more prominent than the other major lines in the hand, physical activities will take precedence over intellectual pursuits.

A WEAK LIFE LINE
A life line may be weak either because it is poorly constructed or because it appears faint or light in comparison to the other major lines. A line that is broken or fragmented along its course denotes a delicate constitution and lowered vitality. A life line that appears fainter than the other lines suggests that its owner is not a great lover of physical activity.

GIVE AND TAKE
In very broad terms, those whose life line forms a wide curve around the thumb are said to be the "givers" in life, while a narrow arc can be a sign of selfishness.

A SHORT LIFE LINE
No other feature in the hand has labored under so much misconception or given greater anxiety than the short life line. True short life lines are extremely rare, although many life lines that appear short are seen. Invariably, in such cases, a close inspection reveals that before its end the line puts out a fine branch that shoots out to the center of the palm and connects with another line. This line represents a new section of life line that takes over from the earlier one. Sometimes, the fate line may do double duty and act as the new section of life line. Essentially, this formation denotes a major, positive change in the individual's life. Settling in a foreign country, marrying a person of another race, or inheriting a fortune are events that may be represented by an apparently short life line.

LIFE LINE
SWINGS OUT

THE LIFE LINE SWINGS OUT
When the life line forms a wide semicircle that sweeps out to the center of the palm it denotes an extrovert and exuberant person. The further out the line sweeps, the more expansive the nature. If you have this type of line you are interested in all that is going on around you. By contrast, a narrow arc indicates a person who prefers his or her own company to that of others.

AMBITION
A life line that begins high up and closer to the base of the Jupiter finger than to the thumb denotes an ambitious individual. Owners of such lines are considered to be good leaders and often attain success in their lives.

ON CLOSE
INSPECTION,
LIFE LINE
CONTINUES

LONG
LIFE LINE

STAY-AT-HOME
A long life line that ends tucked away under the ball of the thumb denotes a love of hearth and home. A life line that sweeps over toward the percussion reveals a love of travel.

PERCUSSION
EDGE

A LONG LIFE LINE
A long life line will not guarantee a long life, but it does show that its owner has considerable physical resources at his or her disposal. Providing the line is unblemished, it suggests that physical effort can be sustained over long periods. The difference between a long life line and a short one is that the owner of the long line possesses greater stamina and resilience.

UPROOTED PAST
A short life line is often seen in the left hand of those whose parents were born in one country but settled in another. On a person who is left-handed the marking will be found on the right hand.

EVENT MARKINGS ON THE LIFE LINE

MARKINGS ON THE LIFE LINE can be divided into two groups: negative and positive indicators. Stars, crosses, islands, and trauma lines fall into the first category. When found in our hands, these markings act either as registers of difficulties or problems that have already occurred, or as warning signs, giving us time to take preventive action before a troublesome event is to take place.

On the positive side, branches that sweep from the life line toward the mounts are considered to represent favorable events. These chart our progress and achievement, pointing out the areas in which we make efforts to improve our condition and status in life.

16TH-CENTURY WOODCUT
This woodcut, showing the life line and fate line, appeared in an early book on palmistry, written by Barthélemy Coclès in 1583.

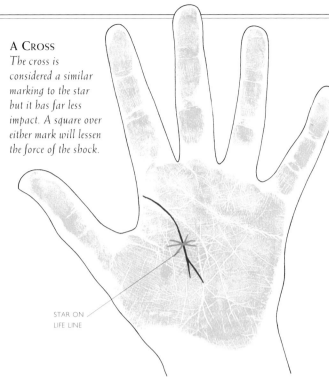

A CROSS
The cross is considered a similar marking to the star but it has far less impact. A square over either mark will lessen the force of the shock.

STAR ON LIFE LINE

A STAR ON THE LIFE LINE

A star is formed by several short bars that intersect each other across the line at one point. It represents a concentration of energy – a sudden surge of power that puts a great strain on your physical reserves. Such a marking is often associated with a shock, whether of a physical or psychological nature. A sudden injury or accident, for example, might well be marked in this way.

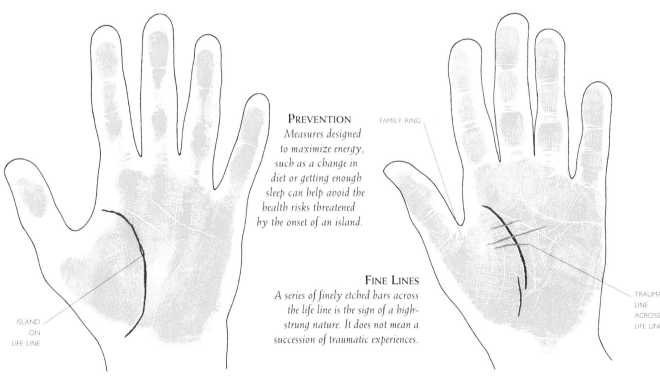

PREVENTION
Measures designed to maximize energy, such as a change in diet or getting enough sleep can help avoid the health risks threatened by the onset of an island.

FAMILY RING

FINE LINES
A series of finely etched bars across the life line is the sign of a high-strung nature. It does not mean a succession of traumatic experiences.

ISLAND ON LIFE LINE

TRAUMA LINE ACROSS LIFE LINE

ISLANDS ON THE LIFE LINE

Because an island essentially splits the line, it points to a period when energy is lowered and resistance is poor. During this time an individual may not feel up to par, and may be more prone to injury or susceptible to any virus that comes his or her way.

TRAUMA LINES ON THE LIFE LINE

Bars that cut through the life line are known as trauma lines and represent emotional upheaval. The severity of the upset is in direct proportion to the length and depth of the line. A line that starts at the family ring suggests worries about a relative.

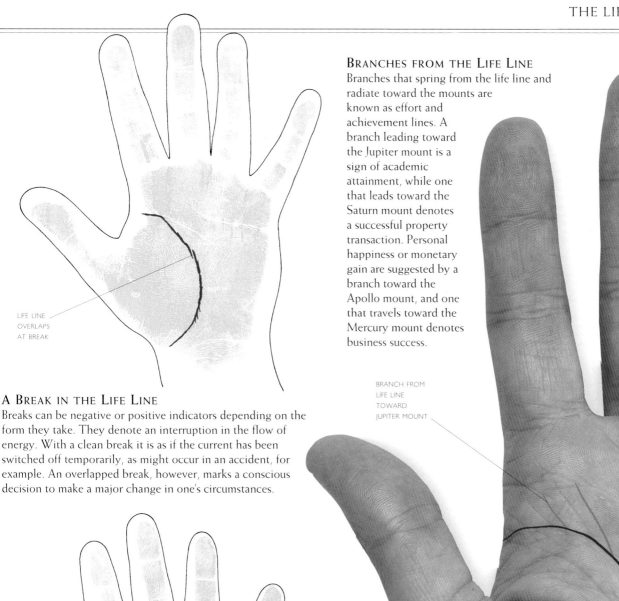

LIFE LINE
OVERLAPS
AT BREAK

BRANCHES FROM THE LIFE LINE

Branches that spring from the life line and radiate toward the mounts are known as effort and achievement lines. A branch leading toward the Jupiter mount is a sign of academic attainment, while one that leads toward the Saturn mount denotes a successful property transaction. Personal happiness or monetary gain are suggested by a branch toward the Apollo mount, and one that travels toward the Mercury mount denotes business success.

BRANCH FROM
LIFE LINE
TOWARD
JUPITER MOUNT

A BREAK IN THE LIFE LINE

Breaks can be negative or positive indicators depending on the form they take. They denote an interruption in the flow of energy. With a clean break it is as if the current has been switched off temporarily, as might occur in an accident, for example. An overlapped break, however, marks a conscious decision to make a major change in one's circumstances.

CLOSE TIES

An adopted child, a grandmother moving in with the family, or even a beloved pet may be denoted by a branch on the inside of the life line.

BRANCH FROM
LIFE LINE TO
LUNA MOUNT

RELATIONSHIP
LINE

MOVEMENT

A branch that shoots out of the life line and sweeps down toward the Luna mount is a sign of movement and travel. The deeper and longer the line, the farther away the individual will travel.

RELATIONSHIPS ON THE LIFE LINE

Branches that peel off from inside the life line indicate relationships. They may signify either a partner or children. Judge by the age and circumstances of the individual to distinguish which type of relationship the branches represent.

HOW TO TIME EVENTS ON THE LIFE LINE

TIMING EVENTS ON THE LINES in the hand is not an exact science. Because hands come in different sizes, it is not possible to have a universal gauge to fit them all. A fairly reliable system exists, but it may require a little adjustment each time it is used. Practice will help to achieve accuracy.

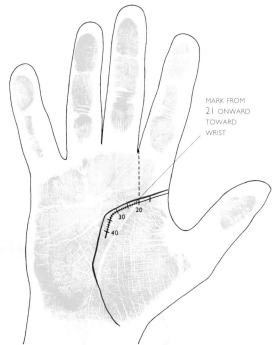

MARK FROM 21 ONWARD TOWARD WRIST

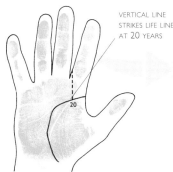

VERTICAL LINE STRIKES LIFE LINE AT 20 YEARS

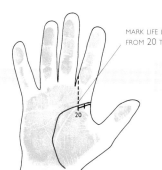

MARK LIFE LINE FROM 20 TO 0

1 On a handprint draw a line from the inside edge of the Jupiter finger down to the life line. This line will strike the life line at approximately 20 years of age.

2 Working from the 20-year mark toward the thumb, mark in the years from 20 to 0 with a sharp pencil, taking 1/25 in (1 mm) to represent one year.

3 If you cannot fit in all the years from 20 to 0, do not worry; it simply means that the life line on the handprint has not printed to the edge of the hand. From the 20-year point, working down toward the wrist, mark in the years from 21 onward on the line. Using a longer dash to mark every 5th and 10th year will make the gauge easier to read.

TIMING A SHORT LIFE LINE

IF YOU HAVE A SHORT LIFE LINE refer to page 55. To time a life line such as this, the procedure is essentially the same as when applying the gauge to a life line of standard length. The vertical line strikes the life line at the 20-year point and years are marked off to the end of the line. At the end of the short line the gauge is transferred to the new line and the timing process is continued.

A LONG OVERLAP

If there is a long overlap between the first part of the life line and the new section, copy the gauge across at the point at which the new section begins. Note the timing of this transfer, for this is when the major life change takes place.

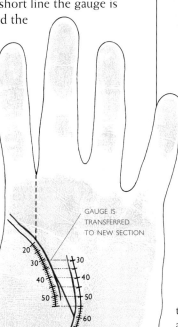

GAUGE IS TRANSFERRED TO NEW SECTION

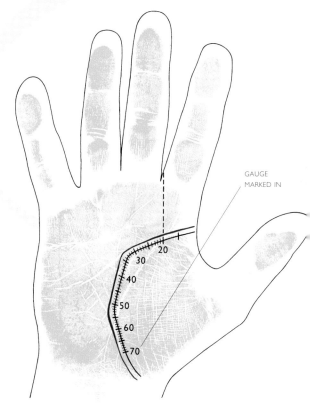

GAUGE MARKED IN

4 As you mark in the years, try not to obscure any features or fine details on the life line itself. Having completed the timing gauge, you are now ready to identify, analyze, and time any past and future events that are registered on the handprint.

TIMING THE LIFE LINE: A CASE HISTORY

BETWEEN THE AGES OF 20 AND 40 is the busiest period in most people's lives. Few people sail through these years without experiencing emotional trauma or facing difficult decisions. Margaret's hand is a prime example, for the concentration of markings across her life line during those years is typical of such eventful times.

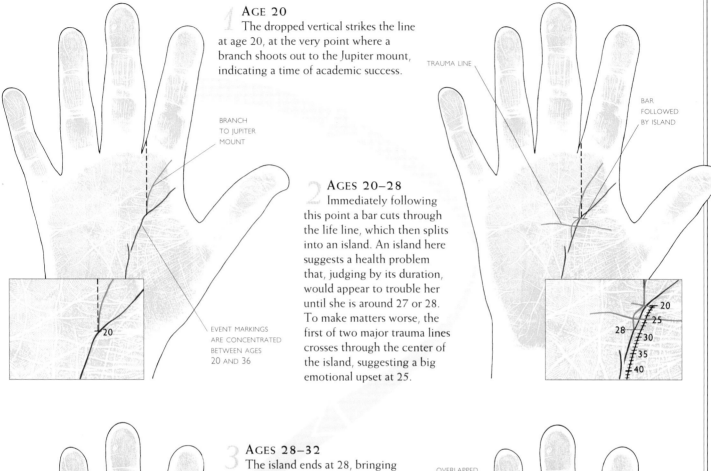

AGE 20
The dropped vertical strikes the line at age 20, at the very point where a branch shoots out to the Jupiter mount, indicating a time of academic success.

BRANCH TO JUPITER MOUNT

EVENT MARKINGS ARE CONCENTRATED BETWEEN AGES 20 AND 36

20

TRAUMA LINE

BAR FOLLOWED BY ISLAND

AGES 20–28
Immediately following this point a bar cuts through the life line, which then splits into an island. An island here suggests a health problem that, judging by its duration, would appear to trouble her until she is around 27 or 28. To make matters worse, the first of two major trauma lines crosses through the center of the island, suggesting a big emotional upset at 25.

20
25
28
30
35
40

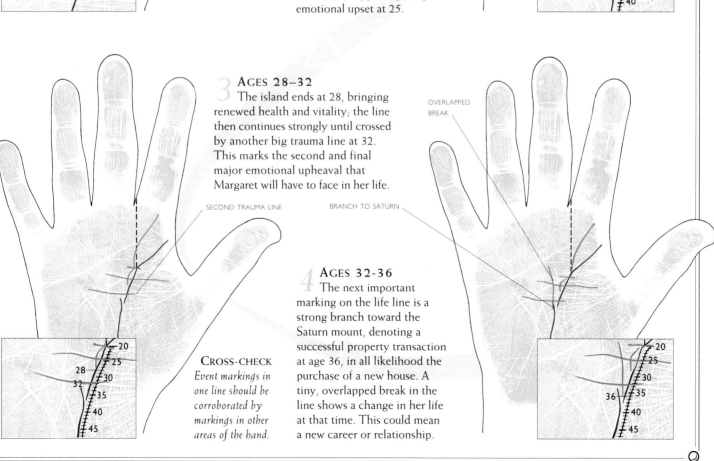

AGES 28–32
The island ends at 28, bringing renewed health and vitality; the line then continues strongly until crossed by another big trauma line at 32. This marks the second and final major emotional upheaval that Margaret will have to face in her life.

SECOND TRAUMA LINE

OVERLAPPED BREAK

BRANCH TO SATURN

CROSS-CHECK
Event markings in one line should be corroborated by markings in other areas of the hand.

20
25
28
30
32
35
40
45

AGES 32-36
The next important marking on the life line is a strong branch toward the Saturn mount, denoting a successful property transaction at age 36, in all likelihood the purchase of a new house. A tiny, overlapped break in the line shows a change in her life at that time. This could mean a new career or relationship.

20
25
30
35
36
40
45

THE HEAD LINE

YOUR HEAD LINE REPRESENTS the way you think and the way you view the world. It describes your mentality and intellectual capacity. It also highlights elements that interest you and that shape your attitudes and understanding of life.

 The construction of your head line – whether it appears strong or weak, its length and breadth, and the direction in which it flows – gives you an accurate reflection of the type of mental energy you possess. Your head line is not a measure of

your IQ; rather, it indicates how you direct your mental energy, how you express your thoughts, and how you apply your talents. Some head lines are long, others are short; some are stronger and deeper than others, some straighter, some more curved. Such diversity reflects the richness and variety of the human mind. Your imaginative and creative potential, your powers of concentration, how you tackle everyday problems, process information, and approach life, are mirrored in your head line.

CHARACTERISTICS OF THE HEAD LINE

MOVING DOWN THE PALM, the head line is the second horizontal crease that lies across it. The line begins on the thumb side of the hand and sweeps out toward

the percussion edge. Some head lines may start attached to the life line, while others are completely separate from it, with a wide gap between the two.

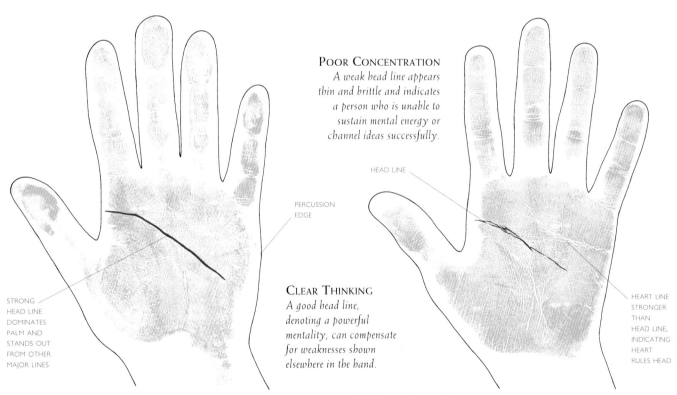

POOR CONCENTRATION
A weak head line appears thin and brittle and indicates a person who is unable to sustain mental energy or channel ideas successfully.

HEAD LINE

PERCUSSION EDGE

STRONG HEAD LINE DOMINATES PALM AND STANDS OUT FROM OTHER MAJOR LINES

CLEAR THINKING
A good head line, denoting a powerful mentality, can compensate for weaknesses shown elsewhere in the hand.

HEART LINE STRONGER THAN HEAD LINE, INDICATING HEART RULES HEAD

A STRONG HEAD LINE
Strong head lines are associated with dynamic thinkers. The stronger and clearer the line, the greater the clarity of thought. Mental processes are sharp, facts are assimilated logically, and decisions that are made rationally work out well. People with strong head lines possess excellent powers of comprehension and the ability to concentrate for long periods of time.

A WEAK HEAD LINE
A weak head line is a sign of a "butterfly" mind and indicates someone who has poor concentration. Common sense may be lacking, for there is a marked tendency to daydream or fantasize, and expectations can be somewhat unrealistic. People with weak head lines can find decisions difficult to make, and may take them from an emotional rather than a logical standpoint.

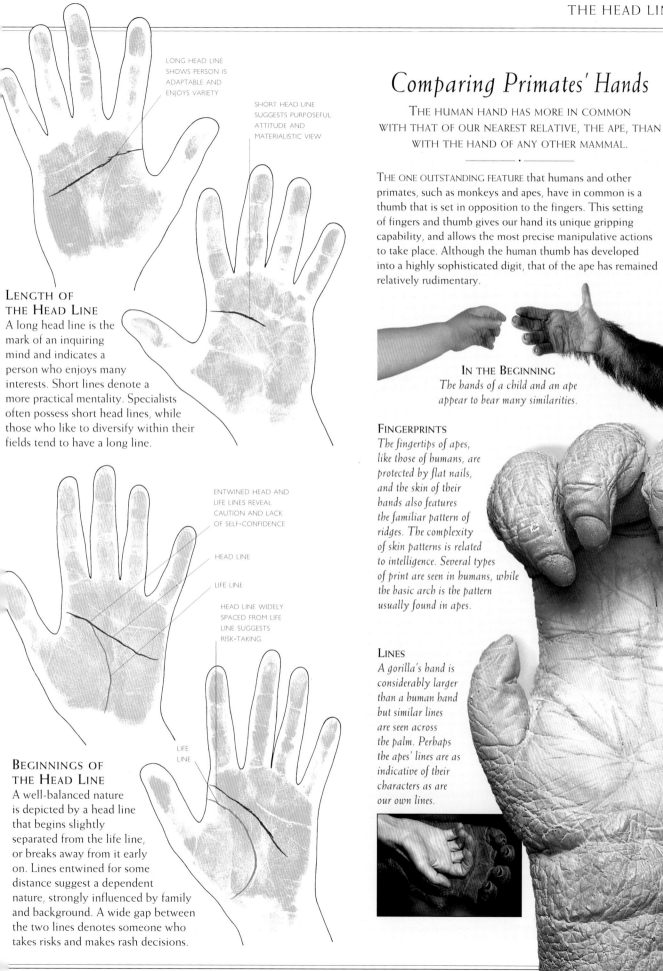

LONG HEAD LINE
SHOWS PERSON IS
ADAPTABLE AND
ENJOYS VARIETY

SHORT HEAD LINE
SUGGESTS PURPOSEFUL
ATTITUDE AND
MATERIALISTIC VIEW

LENGTH OF THE HEAD LINE

A long head line is the mark of an inquiring mind and indicates a person who enjoys many interests. Short lines denote a more practical mentality. Specialists often possess short head lines, while those who like to diversify within their fields tend to have a long line.

ENTWINED HEAD AND
LIFE LINES REVEAL
CAUTION AND LACK
OF SELF-CONFIDENCE

HEAD LINE

LIFE LINE

HEAD LINE WIDELY
SPACED FROM LIFE
LINE SUGGESTS
RISK-TAKING

LIFE
LINE

BEGINNINGS OF THE HEAD LINE

A well-balanced nature is depicted by a head line that begins slightly separated from the life line, or breaks away from it early on. Lines entwined for some distance suggest a dependent nature, strongly influenced by family and background. A wide gap between the two lines denotes someone who takes risks and makes rash decisions.

Comparing Primates' Hands

THE HUMAN HAND HAS MORE IN COMMON
WITH THAT OF OUR NEAREST RELATIVE, THE APE, THAN
WITH THE HAND OF ANY OTHER MAMMAL.

————— • —————

THE ONE OUTSTANDING FEATURE that humans and other primates, such as monkeys and apes, have in common is a thumb that is set in opposition to the fingers. This setting of fingers and thumb gives our hand its unique gripping capability, and allows the most precise manipulative actions to take place. Although the human thumb has developed into a highly sophisticated digit, that of the ape has remained relatively rudimentary.

IN THE BEGINNING
The hands of a child and an ape appear to bear many similarities.

FINGERPRINTS
The fingertips of apes, like those of humans, are protected by flat nails, and the skin of their hands also features the familiar pattern of ridges. The complexity of skin patterns is related to intelligence. Several types of print are seen in humans, while the basic arch is the pattern usually found in apes.

LINES
A gorilla's hand is considerably larger than a human hand but similar lines are seen across the palm. Perhaps the apes' lines are as indicative of their characters as are our own lines.

THE PSYCHOLOGY OF THE HEAD LINE

IF THERE IS ONE LINE in your hand that captures the essential you, it is your head line. It is here that your fundamental psychological disposition is revealed. Head lines can vary considerably both in their length and strength. Whether the line is long or short, shallow or deeply etched, fine in texture or robust, gives valuable clues about your mentality.

The course that the line takes across your palm pinpoints how you think and what you think about. The head line demonstrates the way you tackle problems and how you channel your interests and develop your intelligence through life.

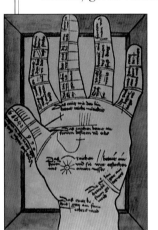

MEDIEVAL PALMISTRY
A hand-colored woodcut from the earliest printed book on palmistry, Die Kunst Ciromantia, *written by Johann Hartlieb in 1475.*

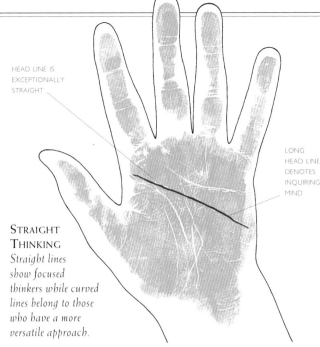

HEAD LINE IS EXCEPTIONALLY STRAIGHT

LONG HEAD LINE DENOTES INQUIRING MIND

STRAIGHT THINKING
Straight lines show focused thinkers while curved lines belong to those who have a more versatile approach.

A STRAIGHT HEAD LINE
A line so straight that it could almost have been drawn with a ruler denotes a pragmatic and analytical mentality. Possessing this line suggests that a person is likely to be practical and logical, and have good powers of concentration. They will have a clear focus on the job at hand and will not be distracted. An aptitude for mathematics, science, technology, and business as well as manual and practical subjects is associated with this line.

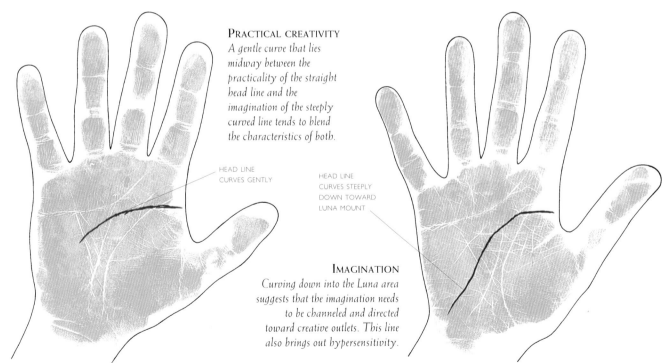

PRACTICAL CREATIVITY
A gentle curve that lies midway between the practicality of the straight head line and the imagination of the steeply curved line tends to blend the characteristics of both.

HEAD LINE CURVES GENTLY

HEAD LINE CURVES STEEPLY DOWN TOWARD LUNA MOUNT

IMAGINATION
Curving down into the Luna area suggests that the imagination needs to be channeled and directed toward creative outlets. This line also brings out hypersensitivity.

A CURVED HEAD LINE
With a gentle, springy curve to the head line, the interests run to more experimental and creative pursuits coupled with a practical bent. People with this line make excellent communicators and may be found in all areas of the media as well as in jobs dealing with the public. Literature and languages, the social sciences, and psychology are also associated with this line.

A STEEPLY CURVED HEAD LINE
The head line sweeping toward the Luna mount brings out creative and artistic talents. The more steeply curved the line, the greater the imagination is likely to be. Painters, poets, and writers do well with this type of head line. However, if the line should penetrate deeply into this area, which represents the subconscious, there is a danger that reality may become blurred.

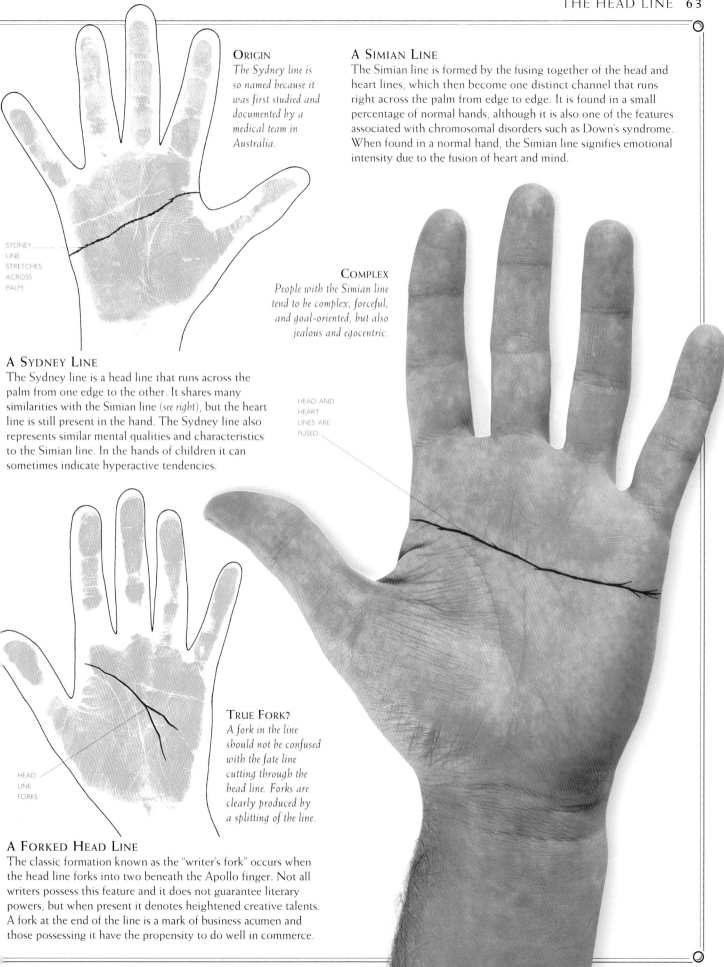

ORIGIN
The Sydney line is so named because it was first studied and documented by a medical team in Australia.

SYDNEY LINE STRETCHES ACROSS PALM

A SIMIAN LINE
The Simian line is formed by the fusing together of the head and heart lines, which then become one distinct channel that runs right across the palm from edge to edge. It is found in a small percentage of normal hands, although it is also one of the features associated with chromosomal disorders such as Down's syndrome. When found in a normal hand, the Simian line signifies emotional intensity due to the fusion of heart and mind.

COMPLEX
People with the Simian line tend to be complex, forceful, and goal-oriented, but also jealous and egocentric.

HEAD AND HEART LINES ARE FUSED

A SYDNEY LINE
The Sydney line is a head line that runs across the palm from one edge to the other. It shares many similarities with the Simian line (*see right*), but the heart line is still present in the hand. The Sydney line also represents similar mental qualities and characteristics to the Simian line. In the hands of children it can sometimes indicate hyperactive tendencies.

HEAD LINE FORKS

TRUE FORK?
A fork in the line should not be confused with the fate line cutting through the head line. Forks are clearly produced by a splitting of the line.

A FORKED HEAD LINE
The classic formation known as the "writer's fork" occurs when the head line forks into two beneath the Apollo finger. Not all writers possess this feature and it does not guarantee literary powers, but when present it denotes heightened creative talents. A fork at the end of the line is a mark of business acumen and those possessing it have the propensity to do well in commerce.

EVENT MARKINGS ON THE HEAD LINE

YOUR HEAD LINE acts like a data bank, storing minute details about your moods, your reactions to problems, your intellectual achievements, and your triumphs and tribulations. Here you will find the psychological high spots when thought and action are clear and channeled, and low points when lethargy and depression set in.

Locked within the strands of your head line are detailed markings that, when decoded, will enable you to pinpoint with great accuracy events and occurrences that have taken place in the past, and which have directly led to the situations in which you find yourself at present.

In addition, markings in this line can give you a glimpse of trends, events, and situations that are likely to happen to you in the future. By learning how to time these markings you will be able to chart your own intellectual progress and development throughout life, and keep one step ahead of the changes that are in store for you.

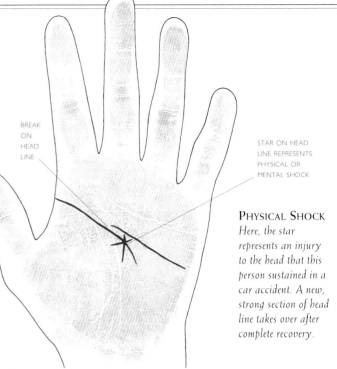

BREAK ON HEAD LINE

STAR ON HEAD LINE REPRESENTS PHYSICAL OR MENTAL SHOCK

PHYSICAL SHOCK
Here, the star represents an injury to the head that this person sustained in a car accident. A new, strong section of head line takes over after complete recovery.

BREAKS AND STARS ON THE HEAD LINE
Stars and breaks on your head line represent events that could have either a psychological or physiological cause. Breaks in the line can indicate either a complete change of attitude or way of life, or an injury to the head. Similarly, stars may represent an actual physical shock or a wonderful surprise.

INTOLERANCE OF STRESS
A single island on the line beneath the Saturn finger denotes an inability to work under stressful conditions.

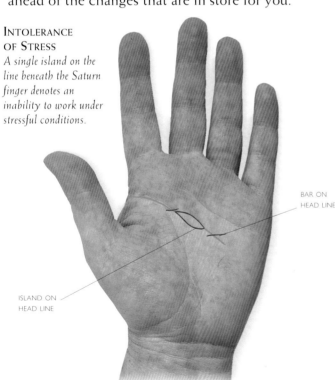

BAR ON HEAD LINE

ISLAND ON HEAD LINE

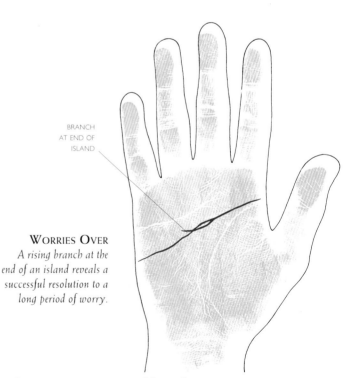

BRANCH AT END OF ISLAND

WORRIES OVER
A rising branch at the end of an island reveals a successful resolution to a long period of worry.

BARS AND ISLANDS ON THE HEAD LINE
A bar cutting through the head line blocks the energy flow, and represents a temporary obstacle such as financial difficulty or a work problem. Times of worry are often denoted by islands. The longer the island, the longer it may take to get over the problem. The duration of islands can be timed accurately (*see page 65*).

BRANCHES FROM THE HEAD LINE
Branches from the head line that point downward denote a time of depression; upward branches signal achievement. Branches to the Jupiter finger denote social or academic achievements; to the Saturn finger, career or property; to the Apollo finger, self-fulfillment; and to the Mercury finger, financial success.

The Rivers of Life

THE LINES AND BRANCHES IN OUR PALMS CAN BE LIKENED
TO RIVERS AND THEIR TRIBUTARIES.

——————— • ———————

ANALOGOUS TO RIVERS that carry life-giving waters across the earth, our palmar lines represent conduits of energy that wash across the map of our hands. And just as the rivers may be clear or muddy, deep or shallow, fast-flowing or sluggish according to the course and structure of their beds, so the quality of our energies is mirrored in our hands in the formation of the lines. Deeply etched lines unimpeded by damlike cross bars mean the current flows freely. Obstructed or islanded lines, however, suggest that energy is intermittent.

SIDETRACKED ENERGY
Branches on the palmar lines, like tributaries of a river that irrigates the surrounding land, carry the influence of the lines to other areas in the hand.

TIMING THE HEAD LINE

THE EVENTS ON YOUR HEAD LINE may be plotted on a time scale. Unfortunately, there is no standard timing gauge that will fit every hand whatever its size. However, once you have learned the basic principles, you can adapt the scale by stretching the measurements a little for larger hands and contracting the gauge slightly for smaller ones. Practicing on friends and relatives will soon make you adept at adjusting the scale to suit all sizes of hands.

APPLYING THE TIMING GAUGE
In the handprint of a journalist, below, the first significant marking on the head line after the 20-year mark is the positive sign of a branch rising toward the Saturn finger. In this case it denotes a satisfactory property deal. At age 30, a cross bar reveals that the subject encountered a stumbling block in her work, and the island that follows shows a setback to her career as a result. The duration of the island can be timed to roughly six years, highlighting the length of time the subject can expect to feel the effects of these difficulties. At age 36, three features occur in this line that help to resolve the problem. First, the island ends. Second, a branch rises toward the Apollo finger indicating self-fulfillment, and third, the head line emerges more robust than before. In fact, this subject found a new job that brought her success through her writing. She consequently gained new confidence in her work, which is indicated by the strengthened head line.

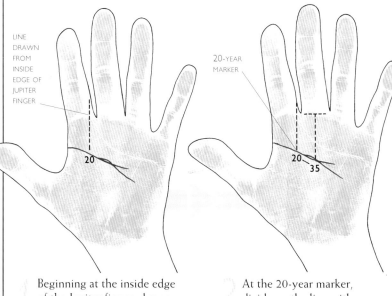

LINE
DRAWN
FROM
INSIDE
EDGE OF
JUPITER
FINGER

20

20-YEAR
MARKER

20
35

BRANCH TOWARD APOLLO
FINGER SHOWS SELF-FULFILLMENT

CROSS
BAR

ISLAND

36
20 25 30 35

Beginning at the inside edge of the Jupiter finger, draw a vertical line down the palm print until you make contact with the head line. This point on the head line is the 20-year mark. From the thumb edge of the hand to this mark represents the first 20 years of the subject's life. You can mark these years in if you wish.

At the 20-year marker, divide up the line with a sharp pencil using about ⅕ in (1 mm) per year. To ensure accuracy, drop another line from the center of the Saturn finger to the head line. This point will mark 35 years. Note that short head lines denote practicality and are not linked to longevity.

THE HEART LINE

T HE KEY TO UNDERSTANDING your emotional responses lies in your heart line. This, the topmost horizontal line in your palm, portrays your innermost feelings, and how you relate to others. By its placement and formation in your hand, your heart line will reveal your sensitivities and emotions, your attitudes in relationships, and your expectations regarding love, marriage, and other emotional partnerships.

Beginning high up in the hand, with its roots in the part of the palm that deals with subconscious communication, the heart line is also an indication of your attitudes to sex and sexuality. These are essential components not only of the giving and receiving of love, but also of personal self-expression and instinctive responses to other people.

Whether you are hot and passionate or cool and detached, whether you are passive and submissive or strong and dominant, whether you fall in love at first sight or take a long and considered view before committing or revealing your affections, whether, indeed, your heart rules your head or your reason stands guard over your emotions will all be revealed by the heart line.

CHARACTERISTICS OF THE HEART LINE

AS WELL AS REPRESENTING LOVE, the heart line can also yield valuable clues about the physiological condition of the heart and blood vessels. Feelings and emotions are represented in its length and direction of travel, while the composition of the line holds information about the body's cardiovascular system.

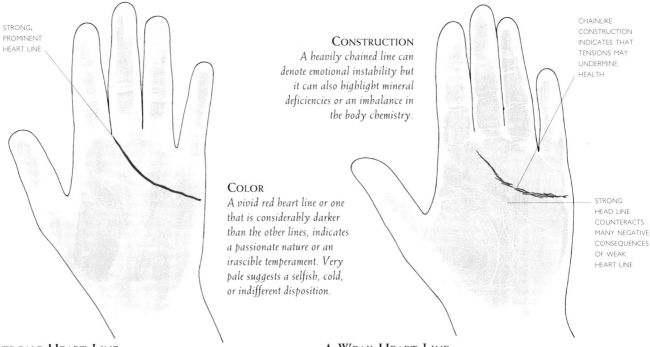

STRONG, PROMINENT HEART LINE

CONSTRUCTION
A heavily chained line can denote emotional instability but it can also highlight mineral deficiencies or an imbalance in the body chemistry.

CHAINLIKE CONSTRUCTION INDICATES THAT TENSIONS MAY UNDERMINE HEALTH

COLOR
A vivid red heart line or one that is considerably darker than the other lines, indicates a passionate nature or an irascible temperament. Very pale suggests a selfish, cold, or indifferent disposition.

STRONG HEAD LINE COUNTERACTS MANY NEGATIVE CONSEQUENCES OF WEAK HEART LINE

A STRONG HEART LINE
If the heart line is clear and deeply etched it reveals a person who is confident of his or her sexuality and is warm and generous toward others. But if this line is the most prominent in the hand, it may indicate that the subject lets the emotional side of their nature govern other aspects of life. People with a dominant heart line tend to act impulsively without thought of the consequences.

A WEAK HEART LINE
Very few people have a perfectly formed heart line, but those whose heart line is weaker than the other lines in the palm – or is poorly formed, heavily chained, or faint – may find emotional involvements prove problematic and unsatisfactory. Insecurity has a tendency to blight emotional relationships. The individual may be easily influenced, and may seek constant reassurance from their partner.

A HIGH- OR LOW-LYING HEART LINE

If the heart line lies very high on the palm it suggests someone who experiences love in an almost spiritual, idealized way. Interactions are emotive, with the individual requiring constant support and attention from his or her partner. A heart line placed lower down the palm brings the emotions into the domain of the head line, and feeling becomes tempered by reason. Such a line would indicate a warm-hearted approach and a more generous nature.

A CURVED HEART LINE

Strong sex drive is associated with a curved heart line. Those who possess it are dominant, demonstrative lovers who prefer to take the lead and invariably make the first move in any sexual encounter. Passionate and vital, physical pleasure is a prerequisite in any intimate relationship they may form.

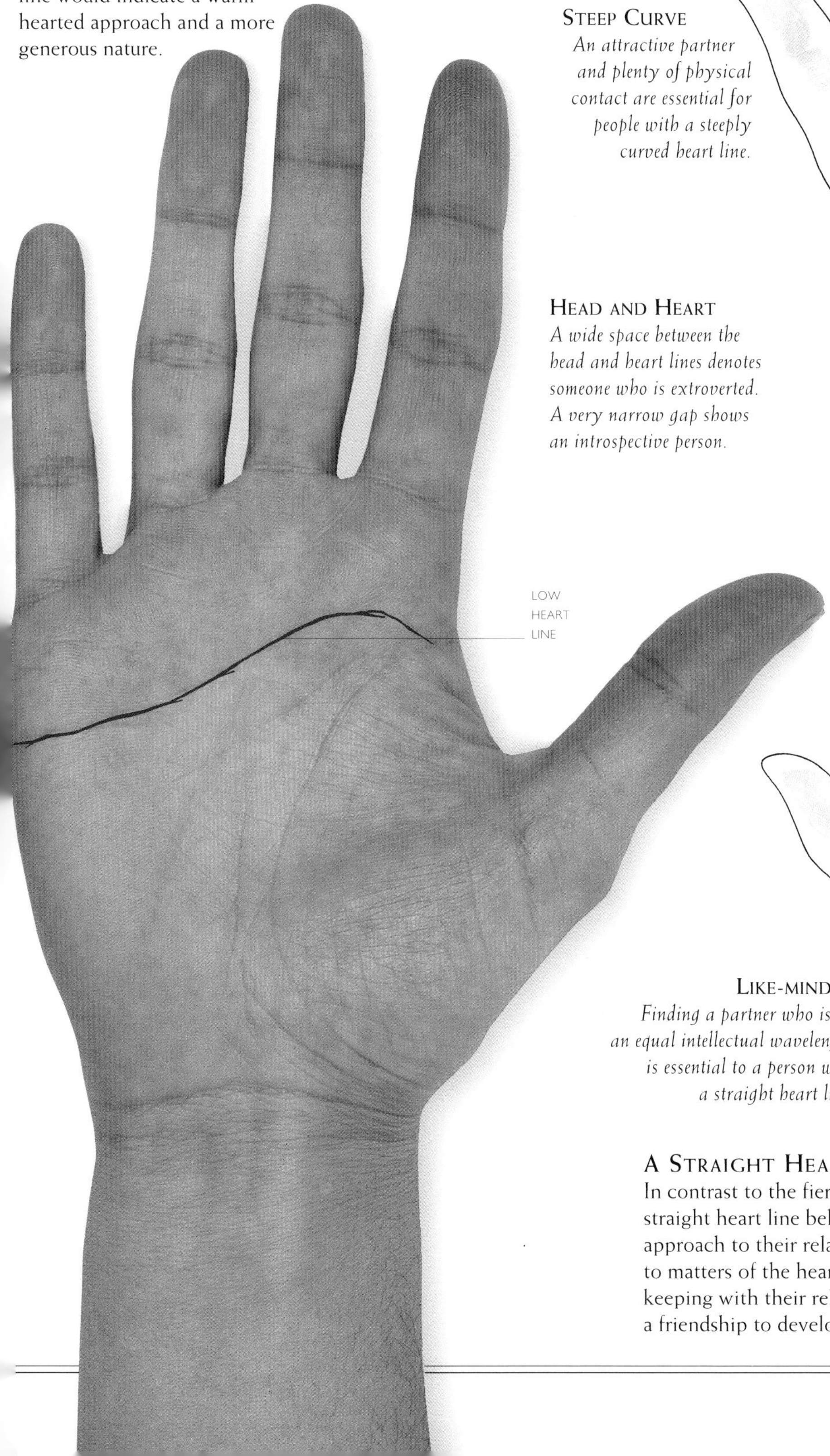

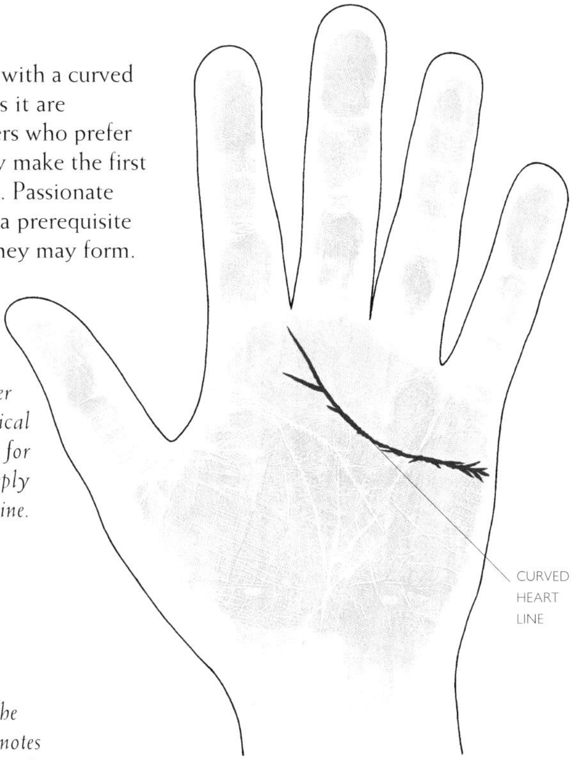

STEEP CURVE

An attractive partner and plenty of physical contact are essential for people with a steeply curved heart line.

CURVED HEART LINE

HEAD AND HEART

A wide space between the head and heart lines denotes someone who is extroverted. A very narrow gap shows an introspective person.

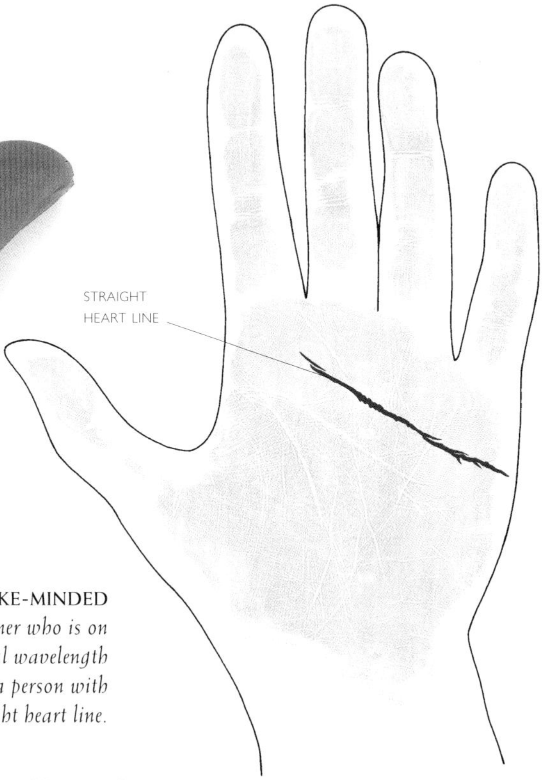

LOW HEART LINE

STRAIGHT HEART LINE

LIKE-MINDED

Finding a partner who is on an equal intellectual wavelength is essential to a person with a straight heart line.

A STRAIGHT HEART LINE

In contrast to the fiery nature associated with the curved line, the straight heart line belongs to those who take a more considered approach to their relationships. They are shrewd when it comes to matters of the heart, and tend not to rush into love affairs. In keeping with their relatively passive outlook, they prefer to allow a friendship to develop before committing themselves entirely.

TYPES OF HEART LINES

WITH VERY FEW EXCEPTIONS, most heart lines begin at the edge of the palm directly beneath the Mercury finger. From here they sweep their way across the top of the palm, the majority ending somewhere below the base of the Jupiter finger, some stretching on to reach the farther edge of the hand, and others falling short and terminating beneath the finger of Saturn.

The composition of your heart line and the place where it ends reveal your emotional behavior. They mirror your sexuality and sexual preferences, and map your capacity to give and receive love.

HEART TO HEART
This cartoon by George du Maurier appeared in Punch, *December 6, 1886. It suggested how hand reading offered scope for harmless flirtation.*

TIMING
The heart line is not considered a reliable line on which to time events. Therefore, applying a timing gauge to this line is not recommended.

HEART LINE ENDS ON JUPITER FINGER

HEART LINE ENDING ON THE JUPITER FINGER
If your heart line sweeps up to touch the base of your Jupiter finger, you tend to be a perfectionist in matters of the heart. You have high standards, and high expectations of those you love. Lovers will be chosen with discrimination, but once you have committed yourself to a partner you will be devoted and true.

ROMANCE
People whose heart lines end on the mount of Jupiter tend to dream of damsels in distress and knights in shining armor.

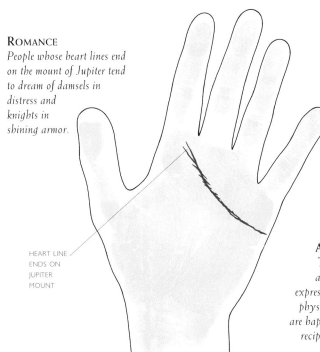

HEART LINE ENDS ON JUPITER MOUNT

HEART LINE ENDS BETWEEN JUPITER AND SATURN FINGERS

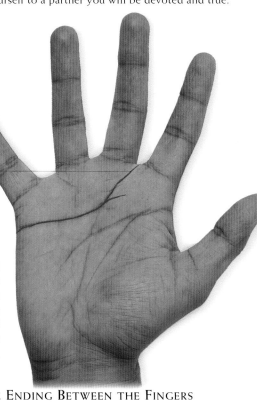

ACTION NOT WORDS
Those possessing this line are people of few words in expressing their love. They are physically demonstrative and are happiest with a partner who reciprocates in the same way.

HEART LINE ENDING ON THE JUPITER MOUNT
If your heart line terminates in the center of the Jupiter mount, you are a consummate romantic. With a rosy aspect on love and an idealistic view of lovers, you have a tendency to put partners on a pedestal. Unfortunately, when you discover that your lover is a mere mortal with feet of clay, you feel disillusioned and betrayed. More realistic expectations are needed to ensure that both you and your partners avoid disappointment.

HEART LINE ENDING BETWEEN THE FINGERS
Reaching up to end on the web between your Jupiter and Saturn fingers tends to be a fairly typical termination of the heart line. If you have this formation in your hand it reveals an affectionate nature and, although you love deeply, you prefer to show how you feel about others – lovers, family, and friends – through the things you do for them rather than by verbal revelations of your love.

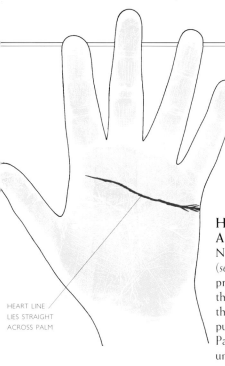

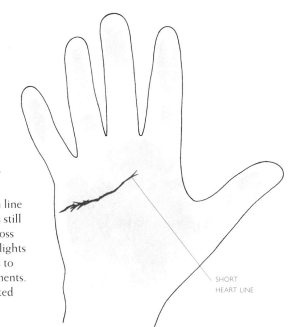

THE ORGANIZER
People who are regularly asked to shoulder responsibilities and invited to join committees almost invariably possess a heart line that travels straight across the palm.

HEART LINE LYING STRAIGHT ACROSS THE PALM
Not to be confused with the Simian line (*see page 63*), because the head line is still present, this heart line stretches across the palm to the thumb edge. It highlights the workaholic, someone who tends to put work before emotional commitments. Partners and family may feel neglected unless time is made for them.

HEART LINE
LIES STRAIGHT
ACROSS PALM

SHORT
HEART LINE

BRANCHES
If your heart line ends in a fork, people will turn to you for sympathy. But if a branch drops down to touch the life line it signifies a disappointment in love.

A SHORT HEART LINE
If a line reaches only as far as the Saturn finger it reveals a person who lacks responsibility when it comes to intimate partnerships. Such people want their fun but not the personal ties and long-term commitment that goes with one-to-one relationships. As far as they are concerned, fleeting affairs are quite satisfactory.

Rings on Their Fingers

FOR MANY CENTURIES RINGS HAVE BEEN USED TO
SYMBOLIZE STATUS AS WELL AS UNITY AND FIDELITY.

—— • ——

A RING WORN ON any finger is significant. One worn on the Jupiter finger highlights the ego and marks a vain and ambitious streak. On the Saturn finger a ring signifies that the wearer has a materialistic attitude. Tradition decrees that the wedding ring is worn on the Apollo finger, since this is linked to the heart and symbolizes the emotions. Rings worn on the Mercury finger are believed to reveal sexual inhibitions.

FORKED
HEART LINE

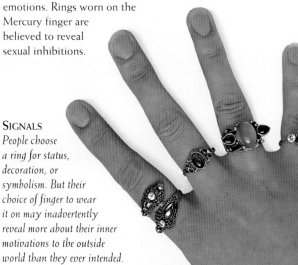

SIGNALS
People choose a ring for status, decoration, or symbolism. But their choice of finger to wear it on may inadvertently reveal more about their inner motivations to the outside world than they ever intended.

HEART LINE ENDING IN A FORK
A fortunate type of heart line to possess is a forked one, because it tends to embrace the qualities of the heart and head. If you have a two-pronged ending, you will be warm and romantic, as well as levelheaded. It is even better, however, if you have a triple-forked ending as this encompasses all the best qualities of the other heart lines shown here. You couple logic with feeling, you are a compassionate listener, and a sympathetic support to your partner.

THE FATE LINE

WHILE YOUR LIFE LINE symbolizes the quality of your life, your head line reveals details about your mentality, and your heart line describes your emotions, it is your fate line that directly relates to your work and the way you deal with your environment. Cutting vertically through your palm, the fate line becomes the linchpin, pulling together all the threads that make up your life and personality. It reveals how you make use of your talents, how you conduct yourself, and the degree of control you are able to exercise over your life and personal circumstances.

In its ideal form, the fate line runs through the center of the palm from the wrist to the base of the fingers, resembling a tentpole rigidly holding upright the structure in which it is placed. However, in these times of social mobility, and changing demands of employment, it is common to find fate lines that are broken, interrupted, or that change direction several times along their course.

The imagery of the tentpole gives a clue to the qualities represented by this line. It describes your capacity for shouldering responsibilities and the way in which the responsibilities are carried out.

CHARACTERISTICS OF THE FATE LINE

IN REALITY, not all fate lines are straight or solid, rodlike formations. Many of them are broken, or composed of a series of overlapping sections. Some begin from a corner of the hand, or have roots in another line. Others may not start until halfway up the palm, and in some hands may not exist at all.

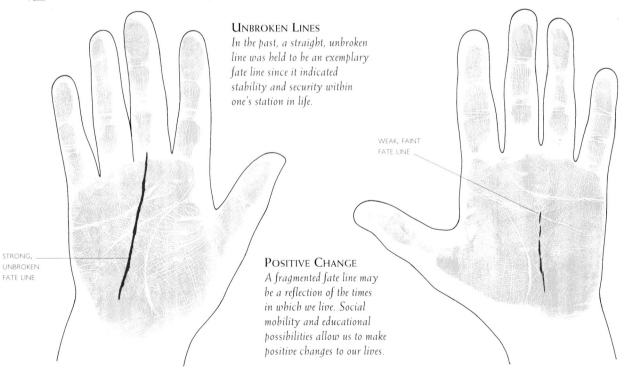

UNBROKEN LINES
In the past, a straight, unbroken line was held to be an exemplary fate line since it indicated stability and security within one's station in life.

STRONG,
UNBROKEN
FATE LINE

WEAK, FAINT
FATE LINE

POSITIVE CHANGE
A fragmented fate line may be a reflection of the times in which we live. Social mobility and educational possibilities allow us to make positive changes to our lives.

A STRONG FATE LINE
A strong, well-constructed fate line is associated with a self-motivated individual, someone with plenty of drive and direction in life. Trustworthiness, qualities of leadership, and seriousness are characteristics of this individual. Such strength of character implies that the person is in control of his or her destiny.

A WEAK FATE LINE
A patchy or fragmented line, faint or poorly constructed, is associated with a lack of direction and an unsettled way of life. Rather than taking control of their own destiny, people with these lines are at the mercy of prevailing circumstances. In time, with positive intentions, weak lines can consolidate and grow stronger.

Asian Hand Reading

HAND READING ENJOYS A MORE CENTRAL ROLE IN
EASTERN CULTURE THAN IT DOES IN THE WEST.

HAND READING IN THE EAST has a much higher profile and a
wider following than in the West, where religion and science
have curbed its progress. Hand readers are consulted on a
regular basis and especially so before any new undertaking,
such as a business venture, a wedding, or the birth of a child.
Also, the actual practice of hand reading differs in emphasis
from that practiced in the West. In particular, the rascettes
and the thumbs are given greater importance.

MARKINGS ON THE PALM
*The greatest difference between hand analysis in the East and West
lies in the importance of the secondary markings, perhaps because
many resemble the ideographic characters of Eastern alphabets.*

NO RULES
*The absence of a
fate line is often
found in the hands
of colorful
individuals who
like to lead
unconventional
lives.*

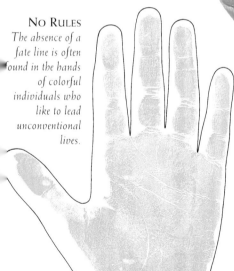

A DOUBLE FATE LINE
Two fate lines are occasionally seen in a hand and the meaning
depends on where along the palm's length the doubling takes place.
If a secondary line follows the main fate line along a parallel course,
the person pursues two separate occupations or careers. A line from
the Luna mount running toward the fate line and then alongside it
denotes a close partner, either in business or emotional affairs.
When short duplicate sections occur, they denote a plurality of
interests, or several
jobs being juggled
at the same time.

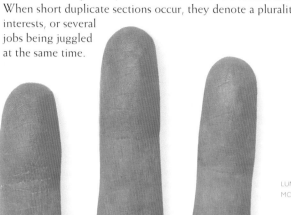

LUNA
MOUNT

DOUBLE
FATE
LINE

DOUBLE FATE
*A parallel fate line
may represent a
husband or wife who is
considered a soul mate,
or it may symbolize a
professional partner.*

NO FATE LINE
When the fate line is missing altogether it reveals a person who
does not want to be weighed down by duty and responsibility,
and who sees little need to put down secure roots in life. Often
these people are nonconformists, rejecting society's values and
making up their own rules. Irresponsibility may be a marked trait.

THE BEGINNING AND END OF THE FATE LINE

RISING VERTICALLY THROUGH THE CENTER of the palm, the fate line falls on the boundary between the conscious and unconscious sides of the hand and therefore symbolizes the individual's ability to synthesize reason and intuition. The way you direct your innate talents, square your personal desires with the demands of society, match your needs to those of others, and find your place in the world at large will all be revealed by the position of your fate line.

In fact, very few fate lines run exactly in a straight line or begin exactly at the wrist to end precisely at the base of the Saturn finger. Although the majority of fate lines do terminate somewhere beneath the Saturn finger, the starting point in the hand differs from person to person. With this line the starting point is as significant as where, and how, the line ends.

FATE LINE STARTING ON THE LUNA MOUNT
Since the Luna mount is the area of the hand that is associated with the imagination, a fate line that begins there suggests interests or a career with a creative emphasis. Dealing with other people or working in the public sphere is also linked with this line.

FATE LINE STARTS ON LUNA MOUNT

LUNA INFLUENCE
Reflecting the social emphasis of the Luna mount, luck and the goodwill of others will play a large role in the successful career of this individual.

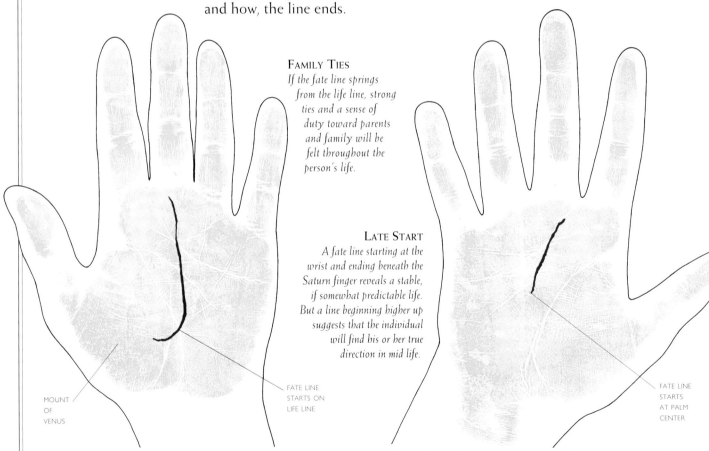

FAMILY TIES
If the fate line springs from the life line, strong ties and a sense of duty toward parents and family will be felt throughout the person's life.

LATE START
A fate line starting at the wrist and ending beneath the Saturn finger reveals a stable, if somewhat predictable life. But a line beginning higher up suggests that the individual will find his or her true direction in mid life.

MOUNT OF VENUS

FATE LINE STARTS ON LIFE LINE

FATE LINE STARTS AT PALM CENTER

FATE LINE RISING FROM INSIDE THE LIFE LINE
When the fate line begins on the mount of Venus inside the life line the family will have been strongly influential in the subject's life. Perhaps they work in the family firm, or their parents set them up in business. A person with a line such as this is also likely to have a strong relationship with his or her own children.

FATE LINE STARTING AT THE CENTER OF THE PALM
When the fate line takes its roots from the center of the palm it suggests that the individual may not quite get into his or her stride until later in life. In middle age the subject is likely to find new direction. It is at the point where the line develops that he or she may find the right career, or settle down in life.

Stigmata

ORIGINATING FROM THE GREEK WORD FOR "SIGN," A STIGMA
WAS A MARK USED TO BRAND SLAVES AND CATTLE.

AMONG CHRISTIANS THE TERM STIGMATA refers to
the marks corresponding to those left by the nails
and spear at the crucifixion of Christ. Devout
believers who have developed the stigmata on their
own bodies are known as stigmatists. They claim
that the marks appear through divine intervention.
Scientists have suggested that it is the religious
fervor itself that somehow induces the physical
changes to occur.

RECENT STIGMATA
*The first and most
famous person to receive
the stigmata was
St. Francis of Assisi
in 1224. Theresa
Neumann (right),
who died in 1962, was
one of the most recent.*

FORKED ENDING ON THE FATE LINE
The fate line deals with duty and responsibility; therefore, its
natural ending is on the Saturn mount. Occasionally, however,
the line terminates in a fork. If the fork branches toward the
Mercury, Apollo, or Jupiter mount it denotes a life and career
blessed with satisfaction and success.

GOOD FORTUNE
*Forks from the fate line to the
Apollo mount can denote either
fame or fortune or both.*

FATE LINE ENDING ON
THE JUPITER MOUNT
The mount of Jupiter is associated
with status and personal standing.
A fate line that swings over to
end on the Jupiter mount is often
seen in the hands of those who
work in high-profile occupations
or who gain power and influence
in their lives and career.

FORKED
FATE
LINE

FATE LINE
ENDS ON
JUPITER
MOUNT

APOLLO
MOUNT

HIGH FLYERS
*Status and prestige,
and a career lived in
the public eye, may be
expected when the fate
line swerves over to end
beneath the Jupiter finger.*

EVENT MARKINGS ON THE FATE LINE

IN THE DAYS when our ancient forefathers believed that our lives were predestined and our lot determined for us at birth, the fate line was known as the line of destiny. Notions that environment plays a large role in shaping our personalities and experiences, and that we are able to make our own choices in life, were not in their scheme of thinking. On the contrary, it was held that the line of destiny was stamped into the hand of the infant, and whatever the line ordained was followed by the individual from the cradle to the grave.

Now, however, we believe that we are constantly shaping our own destiny, although it is for the most part an unconscious process. Signals from our nervous responses and biochemistry form markings in our lines, which may correspond to events taking place years later. Because of this, our fate line will always be several steps ahead of us and thus a herald of things to come.

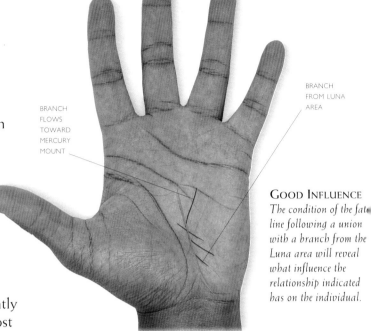

BRANCH FLOWS TOWARD MERCURY MOUNT

BRANCH FROM LUNA AREA

GOOD INFLUENCE
The condition of the fate line following a union with a branch from the Luna area will reveal what influence the relationship indicated has on the individual.

BRANCHES TO AND FROM THE FATE LINE
Branches toward the mounts represent achievement. Toward Mercury, financial success; toward Apollo, personal satisfaction; toward Saturn, material gain; toward Jupiter, status. Branches sweeping from the Luna area to the fate line indicate relationships. Failure to reach the line suggests failed affairs. If a line from the Luna area merges with the fate line it denotes a successful union.

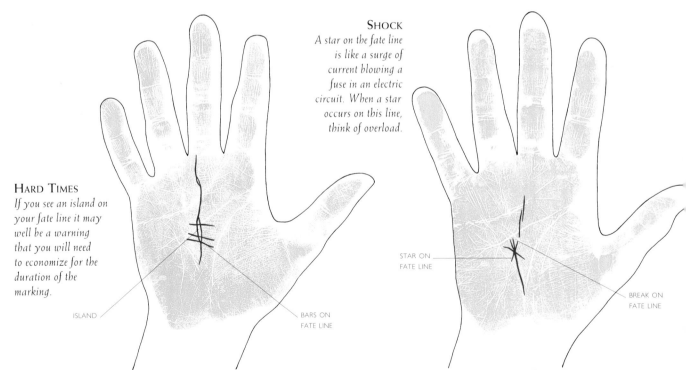

SHOCK
A star on the fate line is like a surge of current blowing a fuse in an electric circuit. When a star occurs on this line, think of overload.

HARD TIMES
If you see an island on your fate line it may well be a warning that you will need to economize for the duration of the marking.

ISLAND

BARS ON FATE LINE

STAR ON FATE LINE

BREAK ON FATE LINE

BARS AND ISLANDS ON THE FATE LINE
A short bar cutting across the fate line represents an obstacle that, although temporary, needs to be negotiated. Your plans may meet with resistance, or a colleague prove difficult. An island is a sign of frustration. It may signal dissatisfaction at work, disenchantment with one's circumstances, or a period of financial restrictions.

STARS AND BREAKS ON THE FATE LINE
A star suggests an experience that makes a sudden impact on the individual's life. It shows a time when a shock or a surprise has overwhelmed the feelings. A break reveals a major change of career or lifestyle. A clean break denotes enforced change, while overlapped ends suggest that the change has been deliberate.

Timing the Fate Line

TIMING EVENTS IN THE HAND is a difficult process since palms come in many different shapes and sizes. A further complication is that the scale on the fate line is more difficult to apply than that of the other major lines. But, once mastered, major turning points or personal milestones that are likely to occur can be pinpointed. The fate line charts our progress through life. Each mark, each break, each deviation corresponds to a specific event that happens to us. By timing this line it is possible to spot a forthcoming change of career, to discover when wedding bells will chime, or when we are likely to expand in business. Similarly, we can be warned about frustrations, disappointments, financial difficulties, and all manner of problems looming over the horizon.

Applying the Timing Gauge

In the woman's handprint below, the section of fate line spanning the years from ages 32 to 51 depicts much activity. Note the doubling of the line denoting the start of a relationship at age 37. At age 42 a cross bar, denoting difficulties, is immediately followed by an island that lasts until she is 51, at which point a new section of fate line starts, suggesting the beginning of a new way of life.

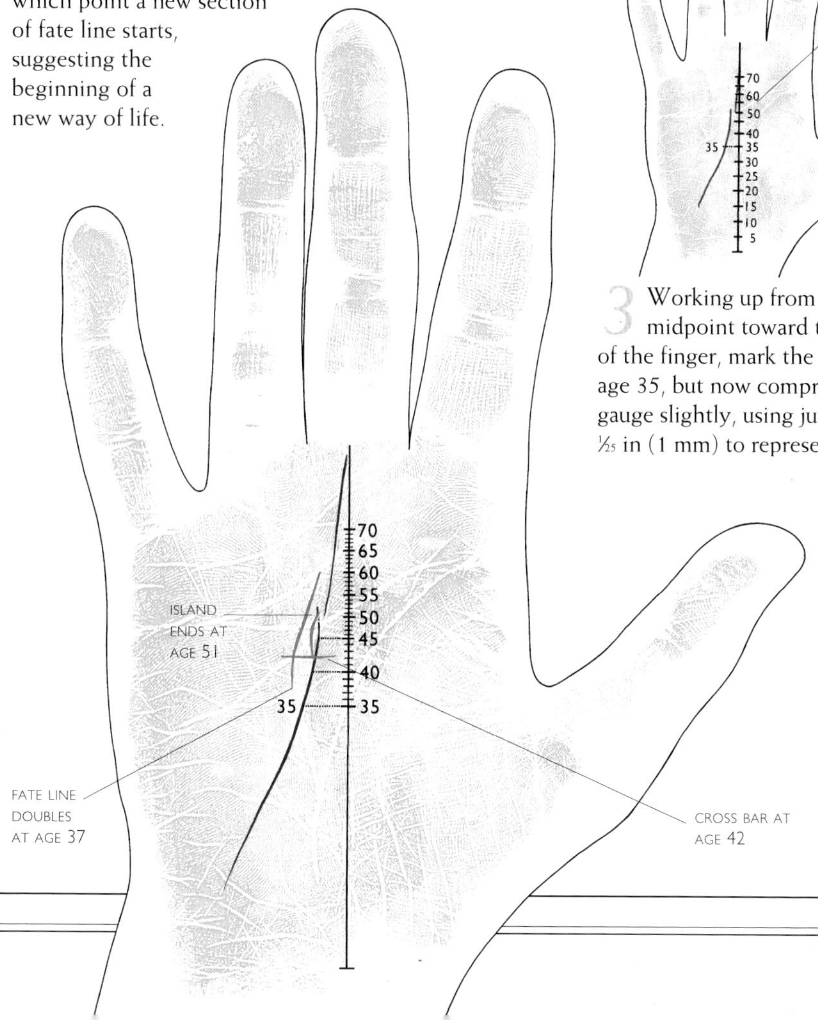
ISLAND ENDS AT AGE 51
FATE LINE DOUBLES AT AGE 37
CROSS BAR AT AGE 42
70
65
60
55
50
45
40
35
35

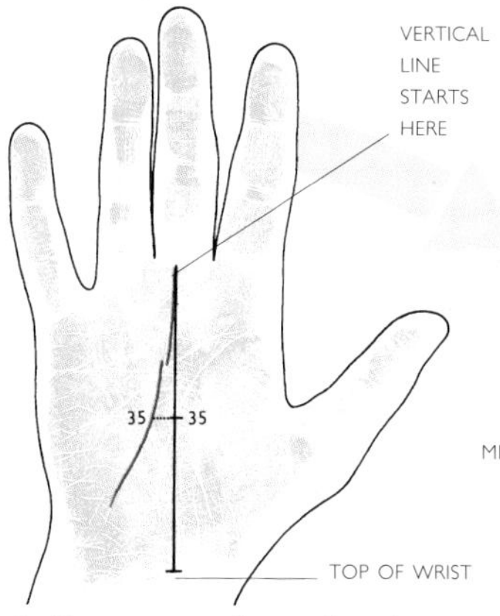
VERTICAL LINE STARTS HERE
35
35
TOP OF WRIST

1 On a copy of your handprint draw a vertical line down from the base of the Saturn finger to the first rascette at the top of the wrist. Measure the line and mark in the midpoint, which represents 35 years of age.

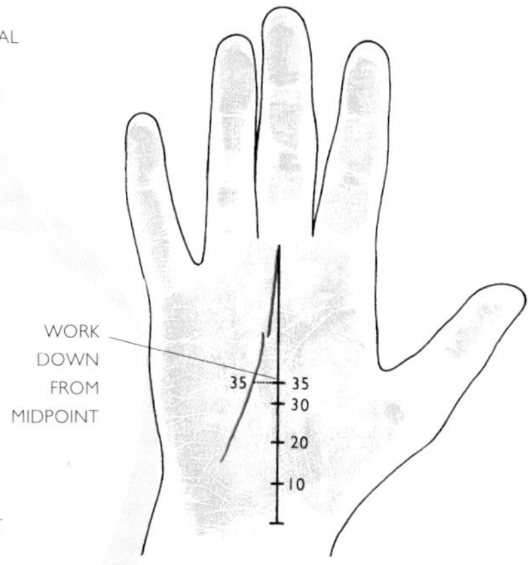
WORK DOWN FROM MIDPOINT
35
35
30
20
10

2 Using 1/25 in (1 mm) to represent one year, start from the midpoint and, working downwards, mark in each 1/25 in (1 mm) to arrive at 0 at the wrist. Adjust the scale if necessary, using slightly more than 1/25 in (1 mm) for a long palm and slightly less for a short one.

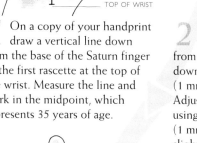

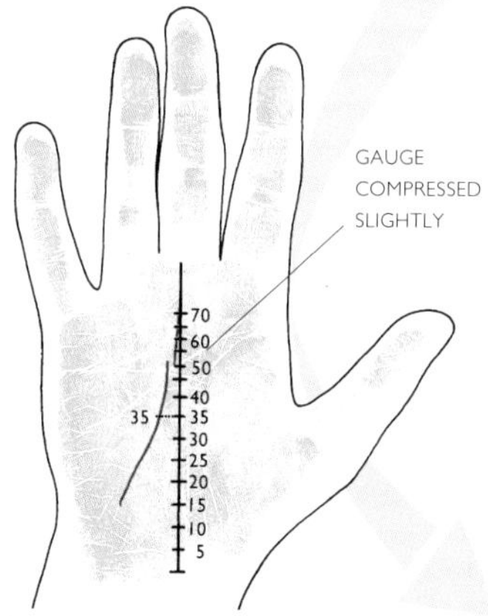
GAUGE COMPRESSED SLIGHTLY
70
60
50
40
35
35
30
25
20
15
10
5

3 Working up from the midpoint toward the base of the finger, mark the line from age 35, but now compress the gauge slightly, using just less than 1/25 in (1 mm) to represent one year.

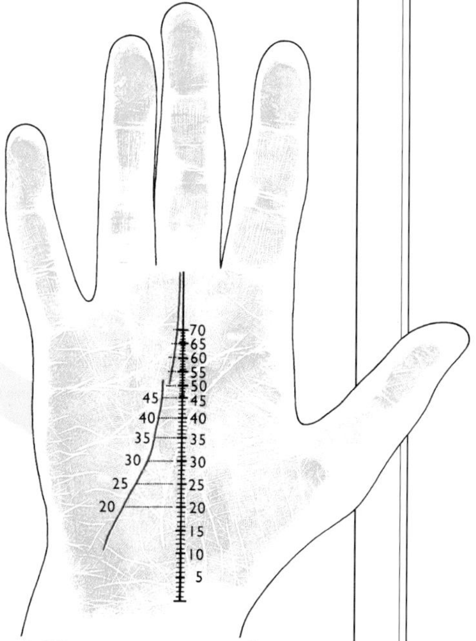
70
65
60
55
50
45
40
35
30
25
20
15
10
5
45
40
35
30
25
20

4 The gauge may now be applied to the fate line. If you draw a horizontal line from any marking on your fate line across to the gauge, you should be able to time events that will take place in your life with considerable accuracy.

DISCREPANCIES BETWEEN HANDS

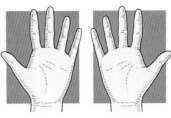

MARKINGS ON the palm differ not only from person to person but from hand to hand. Everyone's hands are unique and not even your right hand perfectly matches your left one. They may look alike and the lines may form similar patterns, but once you start taking a very close look you will notice telltale differences.

It is precisely these differences that bring out the richness and subtlety of an individual's personality. For it is in the discrepancies that

we discover levels of complexity in the personality and pinpoint the disparities between what we feel and how we act. One of your hands reveals your innate characteristics and abilities and the other hand tells you how you have expressed them. If there are major differences between the lines in your hands, it suggests you have either surpassed your initial potential, or, alternatively, that you possess untapped resources that are still at your disposal and which may flourish in the future.

POTENTIAL AND DEVELOPMENT

OUR LEFT AND RIGHT HANDS hold different information. The left presents the inner self and inherited abilities, the right our external facade and the development of

talents (left-handers must reverse this rule). Differences between the hands highlight the exterior versus the personal, and reflect our progress from child to adult.

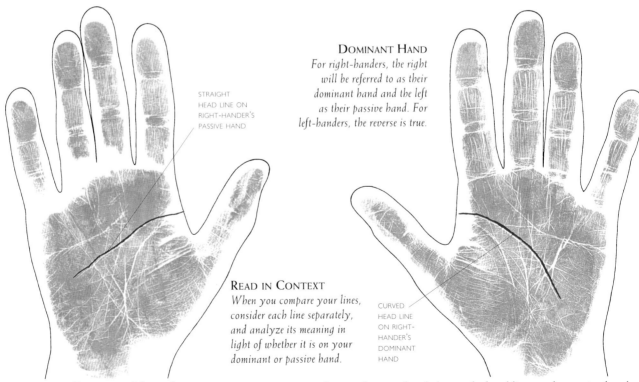

STRAIGHT HEAD LINE ON RIGHT-HANDER'S PASSIVE HAND

DOMINANT HAND
For right-handers, the right will be referred to as their dominant hand and the left as their passive hand. For left-handers, the reverse is true.

READ IN CONTEXT
When you compare your lines, consider each line separately, and analyze its meaning in light of whether it is on your dominant or passive hand.

CURVED HEAD LINE ON RIGHT-HANDER'S DOMINANT HAND

DISCREPANCIES BETWEEN HEAD LINES
Unmatched head lines focus the attention on the development of mentality and intellect. If the dominant hand contains a stronger or longer head line than its counterpart, the individual has made greater intellectual advances than his or her early conditioning might have allowed. If the reverse, true potential

has not been realized. A straight head line on the passive hand with a curved line on the dominant one reveals that a lack of vision in youth has been overcome. Children with straight head lines should be encouraged to broaden their interests in order to be flexible in the future. The reverse pattern implies that early creativity later becomes channeled and structured.

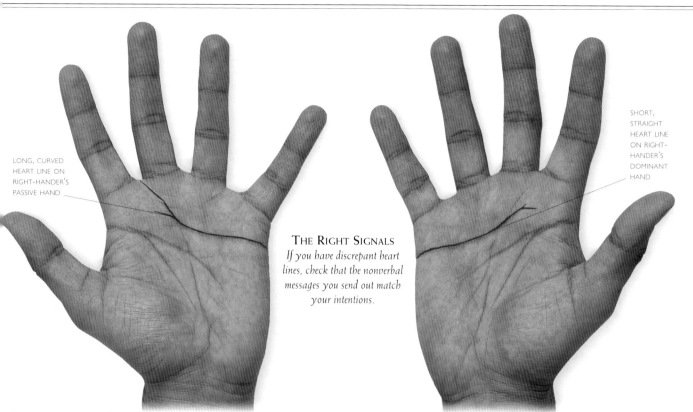

LONG, CURVED HEART LINE ON RIGHT-HANDER'S PASSIVE HAND

SHORT, STRAIGHT HEART LINE ON RIGHT-HANDER'S DOMINANT HAND

THE RIGHT SIGNALS
If you have discrepant heart lines, check that the nonverbal messages you send out match your intentions.

DISCREPANCIES BETWEEN HEART LINES
The heart line represents our emotional nature and how we relate to others, so any variations between the lines in our left and right hands will reveal a disparity between our instinctive innermost feelings and the way we project those feelings to the outside world.

Identifying a disparity between heart lines can often help to explain why misunderstandings occur within a relationship. For example, a curved heart line in the passive hand teamed with a straight one in the dominant hand implies that a soft, romantic nature is hidden behind a tough façade of cool-blooded independence.

DISCREPANCIES BETWEEN FATE LINES
The fate line charts our progression through life, so a discrepancy between the hands reveals your attempts to control your destiny. For example, a weak fate line on the passive hand coupled with a strong line on the dominant hand suggests that a lack of self-confidence has been conquered by adopting a positive attitude.

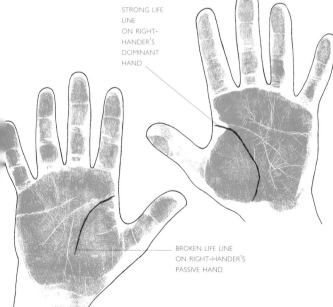

STRONG LIFE LINE ON RIGHT-HANDER'S DOMINANT HAND

BROKEN LIFE LINE ON RIGHT-HANDER'S PASSIVE HAND

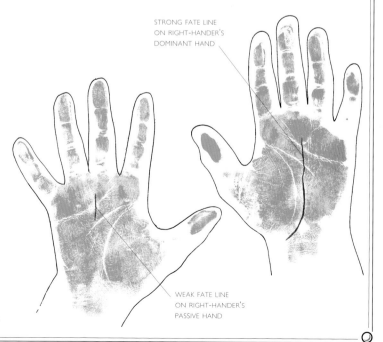

STRONG FATE LINE ON RIGHT-HANDER'S DOMINANT HAND

WEAK FATE LINE ON RIGHT-HANDER'S PASSIVE HAND

DISCREPANCIES BETWEEN LIFE LINES
Mismatched life lines reveal information about health or lifestyle. A short or broken line on the passive hand teamed with a long, strong one on the dominant hand show that potential poor health has been averted. If only your dominant hand has a broken line it suggests that your lifestyle may have adversely affected your health.

THE APOLLO LINE

SOMETIMES KNOWN as the line of the sun, the Apollo line measures the inner contentment we feel throughout our lives. The line is not present in every hand, but when it does appear it is a sign of happiness achieved through success. It represents our capacity to enjoy life and our ability to derive satisfaction from our work. In short, it symbolizes the feel-good factor in us all.

In the past it was thought that the presence of the Apollo line guaranteed fame and fortune, and that its owner could expect happiness and success in abundance. Today's analysts, however, associate the Apollo line with creative talent rather than celebrity and wealth. Certainly, the line is almost always evident in the hands of creative and talented people. And although many of them are rewarded financially for their talent, it is, essentially, the degree of personal fulfillment that the individual obtains through the expression of his or her talents that is represented by the Apollo line.

CHARACTERISTICS OF THE APOLLO LINE

LIKE THE FATE LINE, the Apollo line may commence from different points in the palm. It is rare to find one taking root from the mount of Luna; more usually they begin higher up in the palm and most appear as short sections above the heart line. Wherever it begins, the termination point for this line is on the Apollo mount.

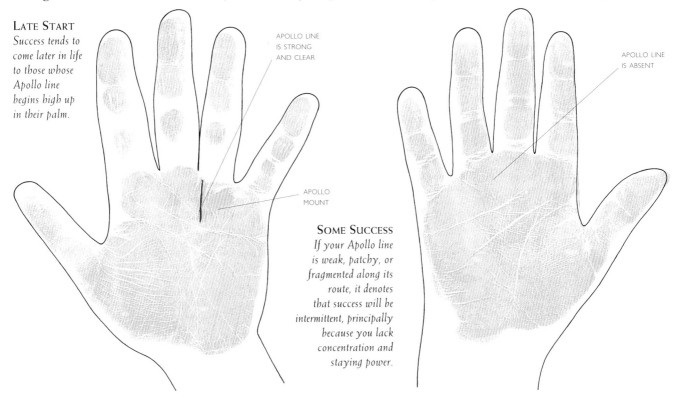

LATE START
Success tends to come later in life to those whose Apollo line begins high up in their palm.

APOLLO LINE IS STRONG AND CLEAR

APOLLO MOUNT

APOLLO LINE IS ABSENT

SOME SUCCESS
If your Apollo line is weak, patchy, or fragmented along its route, it denotes that success will be intermittent, principally because you lack concentration and staying power.

A STRONG APOLLO LINE
A prominent Apollo line is the mark of a charismatic personality. The character is charming, the disposition sunny and outgoing. The longer the line, the more Lady Luck smiles upon its owner, and though undoubtedly born talented, the individual often attains success by simply being in the right place at the right time.

A WEAK OR ABSENT APOLLO LINE
Not all hands possess an Apollo line and some people may have only a very weak or faint one. This does not imply a lack of talent, nor that the individual is doomed to penury. However, an absent or very weak line does suggest a certain cynicism or lack of satisfaction; perhaps a feeling that happiness is just out of reach.

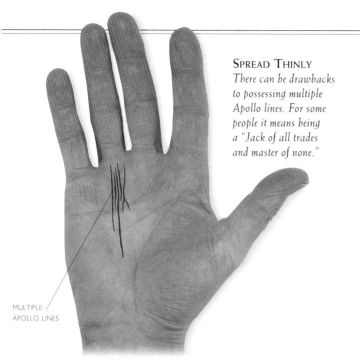

SPREAD THINLY
There can be drawbacks to possessing multiple Apollo lines. For some people it means being a "Jack of all trades and master of none."

MULTIPLE
APOLLO LINES

MULTIPLE APOLLO LINES
In some hands a cluster of Apollo lines may be seen. A bundle such as this represents a versatile, multitalented individual, someone who is accomplished in several different areas and who has the potential to achieve satisfaction and success through the application of one or all of his or her talents.

The Hand in Shiatsu
IN THE JAPANESE PRACTICE OF SHIATSU, FINGER PRESSURE IS USED TO STIMULATE THE CHANNELS OF ENERGY AND RESTORE BALANCE IN THE BODY.

AT BIRTH, THE BODY IS THOUGHT to be in equilibrium, but stresses in life throw that natural balance out of kilter. *Jitsu*, or excessive energy in one organ leads to *kyo*, or depletion of energy elsewhere, an imbalance that is believed to lead to poor health. Specific points on the hand are directly linked to internal organs. Applying pressure to these points releases blocked energy and rebalances the system.

PRESSURE POINTS
Points of the hand are linked to specific internal organs.

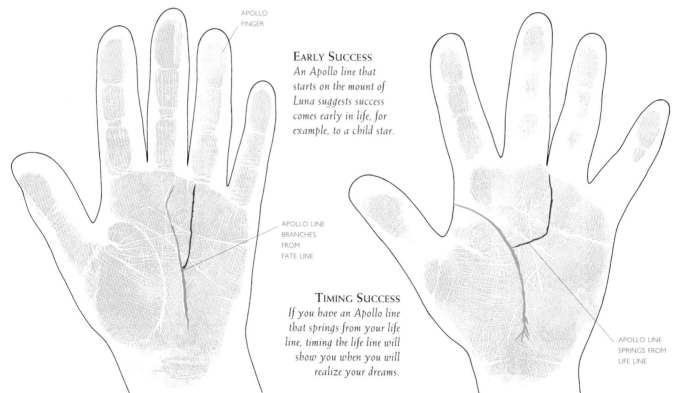

APOLLO
FINGER

EARLY SUCCESS
An Apollo line that starts on the mount of Luna suggests success comes early in life, for example, to a child star.

APOLLO LINE
BRANCHES
FROM
FATE LINE

TIMING SUCCESS
If you have an Apollo line that springs from your life line, timing the life line will show you when you will realize your dreams.

APOLLO LINE
SPRINGS FROM
LIFE LINE

APOLLO LINE BRANCHING FROM THE FATE LINE
A common form of the Apollo line is one that branches out from the fate line and rises up toward the Apollo finger. This denotes that the individual's talents become recognized from the moment the Apollo line springs out from the fate line. It also suggests that success is achieved through the person's own merit and hard work.

APOLLO LINE BRANCHING FROM THE LIFE LINE
An Apollo line that sweeps out from the life line is a rare find. When it exists it denotes that the owner achieves prosperity through his or her own efforts. If the line actually takes root from inside the life line, or from the mount of Venus, it may suggest that money or property comes via the family.

EVENT MARKINGS ON THE APOLLO LINE

BECAUSE THE APOLLO LINE symbolizes our sense of fulfillment and the satisfaction we feel in our lives, any markings on this line will reflect on events that specifically influence or alter our happiness and well-being. As with all markings on the lines, they fall into negative and positive categories. However, because the line itself is a measure of how good we feel about ourselves – about our lives, about those we love, and our standing and reputation – markings on it are, in the main, negative, diminishing our joy of life.

Curiously, a star, the one marking that on any other line is considered to be a harbinger of misfortune, is an augury of brilliant success when it appears on the Apollo line.

APOLLO
In legend, Apollo was the name given to the sun god. He ruled over creativity, especially music and the arts.

LUCK ON THE LOTTERY
Winning a substantial sum of money in a national lottery is the sort of event that would be marked by a star on the Apollo line.

STAR ON APOLLO LINE

A STAR ON THE APOLLO LINE
On the line of Apollo, the star loses its traditionally negative associations and is instead a mark of splendid good fortune. It depicts that moment when the individual's talents and hard work are acknowledged, or when he or she experiences that feeling of being flushed with success. A sudden stroke of luck, an unexpected windfall, receiving honors or prizes, or attaining overnight success may all be denoted in this way.

BAD PRESS
Traditionally, it was held that an island on the Apollo line represented a scandal in one's life. Today, we interpret the marking as depicting loss of esteem, or a damaged reputation.

ISLAND ON APOLLO LINE

RECOVERY
The strength of the Apollo line after a cross or a bar reveals the effects of the impediment. If the line is strong, no lasting damage has occurred; if weak, confidence has been impaired.

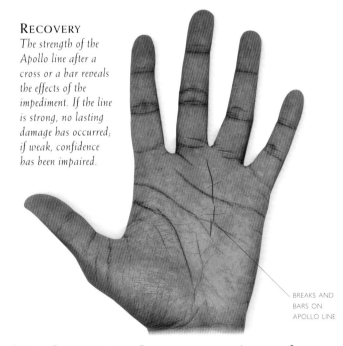

BREAKS AND BARS ON APOLLO LINE

AN ISLAND ON THE APOLLO LINE
Islands always denote a decrease in the power of whatever facet of life the line represents. Here, an island would reflect a temporary loss of the individual's contentment and peace of mind. The marking may represent a period of worry brought on by money problems, or by a loss of honor or prestige. The anxiety can be timed (see page 81) because it lasts for the duration of the island.

BARS, CROSSES, AND BREAKS ON THE APOLLO LINE
On whatever line a bar occurs, it acts as a setback or obstacle. A bar on the Apollo line represents a temporary glitch, a hold-up that impedes progress to success. Two bars forming a cross on the line denotes disappointment or external agents undermining the person's reputation. A break in the line marks a change, ending one venture and beginning something new.

Famous Imprints

MANY FAMOUS PEOPLE HAVE LEFT THEIR "SIGNATURE" ON HOLLYWOOD BOULEVARD.

AUTOGRAPH
Clint Eastwood follows a long tradition, begun on May 17, 1927, of film stars who have made hand- and footprints on Hollywood Boulevard.

LEGEND HAS IT THAT NORMA TALMADGE stepped onto the wet cement in front of the Chinese Theatre on Hollywood Boulevard when it was built by Sid Grauman in 1927. Sid persuaded Mary Pickford and Douglas Fairbanks to repeat the trick with their hands and feet, so beginning the world's largest autograph album. In fact, Sid got the idea from his French stonemason, Jean Klossner, who had "signed" his work with his hand in the cement in the traditional manner.

TIMING THE APOLLO LINE

TO TIME EVENTS THAT are marked on the Apollo line, a similar procedure is followed to that of timing the fate line (*see page 75*). The gauge is marked down the center of the palm and the year markers are transferred across and read off against the Apollo line. Since Apollo lines vary in length, many may not start until halfway up the palm, some only above the heart line.

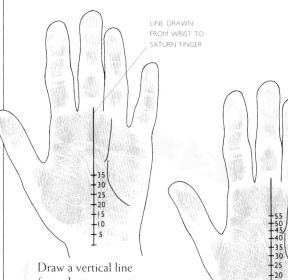

LINE DRAWN FROM WRIST TO SATURN FINGER

HEART LINE

LINE STRENGTHENS AFTER ISLAND

STAR AT AGE 30

LINE DOUBLES AT AGE 39

1 Draw a vertical line from the top rascette to the place where the Saturn finger meets the palm. Find the halfway point and mark that as 35 years. Using ⅕ in (1 mm) to represent one year, and working down the line, fill in the years from the 35-year mark to 0 at the wrist.

2 Working up from 35, mark off subsequent years, but now you must slightly compress your measurements so that just less than ⅕ in (1 mm) will represent one year. Transfer the year markers horizontally across to strike the Apollo line. Remember, the line may not even appear until beyond the heart line.

APPLYING THE TIMING GAUGE
Georgia is a talented fashion designer and highly regarded among her contemporaries. Her Apollo line starts low in her hand, taking its root from the mount of Luna and thus confirming creative talent and imaginative flair. A star on the line spotlights the acclaim she received when, aged 30, she unveiled her first major collection. Nine years later she branched out into a range of cosmetics that was to prove highly successful. The doubling of the Apollo line at age 39 denotes the twin ventures. A break in the line at age 44 marks a departure from designing knitwear to marketing textiles for interior decoration. Rapid expansion and unsound advice, coupled with a disastrous personal relationship, led to the collapse of her business and a precarious financial situation that was to last for almost five years. An island on the line from age 49 to 54 highlights her disappointment and loss of prestige at that time. From her 54th year, the Apollo line strengthens dramatically, revealing a meteoric rise in her fortunes as she successfully relaunched her knitwear designs.

SECONDARY LINES AND PATTERNS

SOME OF THE SECONDARY lines and patterns featured in the following pages are seldom seen, but when they are found they add color and depth to the personality, and they give the hand reader further clues for building a full profile. They can highlight unusual qualities that not only put a slant on the nature and disposition of the character, but which also add to a person's individuality. These minor lines add definition to any analysis of the hand, modifying character traits, refining categories, and spotlighting natural aptitude and particular talents.

Some people have a great many extra lines or patterns, which gives their hands a busy appearance, while others have hands that seem rather featureless, with very few secondary markings. Most usually, people will have one or two, and of all the secondary lines and patterns, it is perhaps the Mercury line, in its variety of forms and permutations, that is most commonly found in people's hands.

ANALYZING THE SECONDARY LINES

WHEN PRESENT, the Mercury line may start on the mounts of Luna or Venus, or spring from the life line itself. Its natural progression is across the palm toward the Mercury mount. The Via Lascivia and the travel lines both lie across the percussion edge of the hand, while Mars lines are freestanding inside the life line.

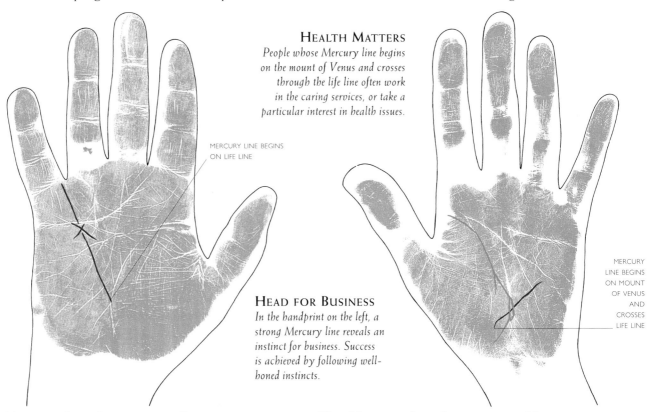

HEALTH MATTERS
People whose Mercury line begins on the mount of Venus and crosses through the life line often work in the caring services, or take a particular interest in health issues.

MERCURY LINE BEGINS ON LIFE LINE

HEAD FOR BUSINESS
In the handprint on the left, a strong Mercury line reveals an instinct for business. Success is achieved by following well-honed instincts.

MERCURY LINE BEGINS ON MOUNT OF VENUS AND CROSSES LIFE LINE

THE MERCURY LINE INFLUENCING BUSINESS
The Mercury line may be interpreted as an indicator of business acumen either when it begins on the mount of Luna or when it springs from the life line. Those who have this marking invariably succeed in business because, being in tune with their intuitive faculties, they bring shrewdness and foresight into their dealings.

THE MERCURY LINE INFLUENCING HEALTH
In the past it was believed that the Mercury line, also known as the Hepatica or health line, indicated poor health, and it was better not to possess the line at all. Modern analysts argue that it is an indicator of personal health. Tiredness, for example, can make the line stronger, while relaxation can make it disappear.

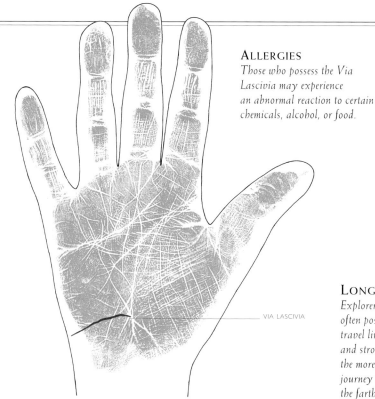

ALLERGIES
Those who possess the Via Lascivia may experience an abnormal reaction to certain chemicals, alcohol, or food.

VIA LASCIVIA

LONG JOURNEY
Explorers and travelers often possess a thicket of travel lines. The longer and stronger each line, the more important is the journey it represents, and the farther you will go.

THE VIA LASCIVIA
Appearing as a horizontal line across the mount of Luna, the Via Lascivia was historically believed to represent wanton behavior. Modern research, however, has discovered a link between the line and sensitivity to allergens. Because of this, the line is now often known as the allergy line.

PERCUSSION EDGE

NUMEROUS TRAVEL LINES

LUNA MOUNT

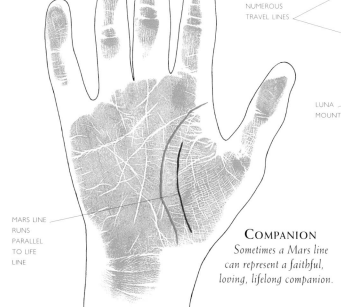

MARS LINE RUNS PARALLEL TO LIFE LINE

COMPANION
Sometimes a Mars line can represent a faithful, loving, lifelong companion.

THE TRAVEL LINES
Voyages, and traditionally those that take you to far-flung destinations, are represented by horizontal lines that enter the palm from the percussion edge and lie across the top of the Luna mount and over the Mars Negative mount. The more lines an individual has, the more of a wanderer he or she will be. Unblemished lines augur safe passage. Those containing islands, bars, or breaks warn of difficulties.

MARS
Mythological god of war, Mars symbolizes dynamic energy and drive. Positively, this manifests itself in courage and endurance; negatively, as aggression and brute force.

THE MARS LINE
Mars lines run inside and parallel to the life line. Some are short while others shadow the life line along its entire course. The Mars line represents secondary protection and extra vitality. When a line runs alongside a break in the life line (*see page 57*) it indicates that, despite health being at risk, physical defenses are shored up.

ANALYZING THE SECONDARY PATTERNS

WHILE EVERYBODY possesses the lines around the wrist called the rascettes, the girdle of Venus and the bow of intuition are far less common. Rarer still are the semicircular line formations that are found around the base of the fingers at the top of the palm.

Though uncommon, these markings are pointers, enhancing or detracting from the qualities that are represented by the areas on which each marking is found. Some are decidedly negative, some positively desirable. Each leads to a greater understanding of the fundamental character of the owner of the palm.

VENUS
Known as Venus to the Romans, and as Aphrodite to the Greeks, this deity was worshiped as the goddess of love.

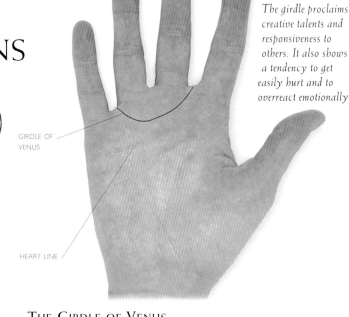

RESPONSIVE
The girdle proclaims creative talents and responsiveness to others. It also shows a tendency to get easily hurt and to overreact emotionally.

GIRDLE OF VENUS

HEART LINE

THE GIRDLE OF VENUS
A fairly rare marking, the girdle of Venus is a semicircular pattern located above the heart line that straddles the middle two mounts. It appears most commonly as fragmented pieces and denotes intense feelings, heightened emotions, and sensitivity. People with this pattern may easily become addicted to stimulants.

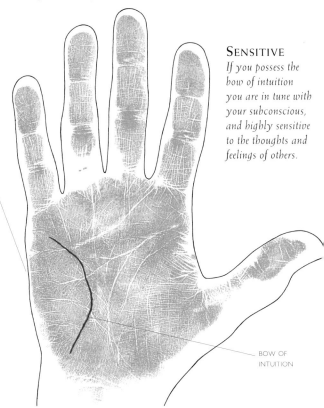

SENSITIVE
If you possess the bow of intuition you are in tune with your subconscious, and highly sensitive to the thoughts and feelings of others.

PERCUSSION

HEALTH
Hand analysts agree that the formation of the top rascette in a woman's hand gives clues about her gynecological health.

BOW OF INTUITION

RASCETTES

THE RASCETTES
Otherwise known as bracelets, the rascettes are the rings at the boundary between the palm and the wrist. Little regard is paid to their meaning in the West, but Asian hand analysts claim they reveal valuable information about length of life. Three strong, unbroken rascettes are said to be a sign of longevity.

THE BOW OF INTUITION
Few hands possess the bow of intuition in its perfect form. The line is found on the percussion side of the palm and appears in the shape of a crescent that starts on the mount of Luna and curves around to end beneath the Mercury finger. People who possess this line are blessed with intuition and acute powers of perception.

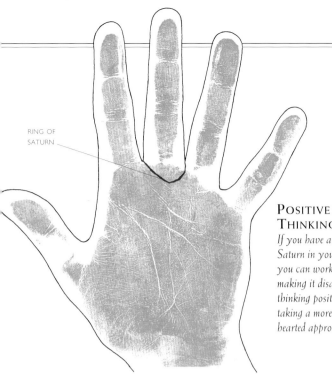

RING OF
SATURN

POSITIVE THINKING
If you have a ring of Saturn in your hand you can work at making it disappear by thinking positively and taking a more light-hearted approach to life.

THE RING OF SATURN
The ring of Saturn, an arc formation encircling the root of the Saturn finger, is the classic symbol of the "wet-blanket," or party-pooper. Fortunately, it is seldom found and rarely occurs as a complete semicircle. A lack of *joie de vivre* accompanies this pattern, along with a jaundiced eye and a melancholic frame of mind.

CREATIVE PURSUITS
The ring of Apollo can be made to disappear with a positive attitude. Taking opportunities to participate in cultural activities may encourage artistic inspiration.

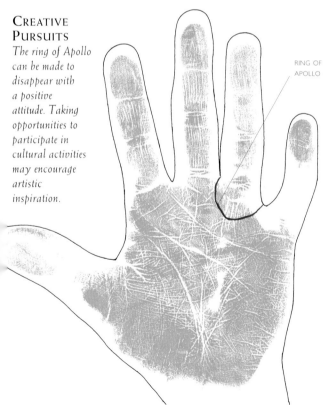

RING OF
APOLLO

THE RING OF SOLOMON
Sometimes occurring as an almost straight line and at other times as a semicircle, the ring of Solomon is found on the mount at the root of the Jupiter finger. Associated with the fabled judgment of Solomon, when found it represents wisdom and philosophical understanding. Those who possess this mark make fine teachers, lawyers, and judges. It is often found in the hands of people who are highly respected and in positions of authority.

RING OF
SOLOMON

WISDOM
The ring of Solomon is also known as the ring of Jupiter. If you possess this mark you have what is known as an old head on young shoulders.

THE RING OF APOLLO
A ring on the Apollo mount encircling the Apollo finger is very rare, and perhaps just as well, because when present the marking seems to act as a block, frustrating the natural spontaneity and optimism of the individual. Aesthetic appreciation may be poorly developed and creative expression is held in check.

APPLIED HAND ANALYSIS

*Our hands contain a wealth of information about ourselves —
our desires and motivations, our likes and dislikes, our
way of interacting with others, our likely behavior in certain
situations, and how we may react to different events. All we
need to do is learn how to decipher the clues.*

INTRODUCING HAND ANALYSIS • RELATIONSHIPS
COMPATIBILITY • THE FAMILY • OCCUPATIONS • HEALTH
MONEY AND LUCK • TRAVEL AND MOVEMENT
RETIREMENT • GROWTH AND CHANGE

INTRODUCING HAND ANALYSIS

GONE ARE THE DAYS of crossing the gypsy's palm with silver. Today's hand reader is a sophisticated practitioner who often works from a modern office and is consulted by people requiring guidance on a wide range of life issues. People might approach a hand reader for assistance in problem-solving, enlightenment on a situation, an objective confirmation of life decisions, or to gain self-knowledge and information about their path in life. Whatever the questions, the analyst should be able to offer constructive advice and show a choice of directions in which to travel.

Modern Hand Analysis

Hand reading has evolved over thousands of years. A body of knowledge, based on observation, has matched behavior and events to corresponding patterns and markings in the hand. Modern hand analysts have distilled the most relevant correlations and blended them with our understanding of the psychology of the individual.

This valuable analytical technique can help to unravel the complexities of the human psyche. Clues are gathered from the palms and fingers, and each clue is corroborated and refined against the other. They are then pieced together, somewhat like a jigsaw puzzle, until the emerging portrait of the individual is complete.

Step-by-step Assessment

The first step of the investigation includes the physical aspects of the hand: the appearance and texture, the shape, the construction of the mounts and digits, and whether the hand is used with extroverted gestures or reserved self-control. The second step takes into account the skin markings that form the patterns on the digits and palms. These markings are a register of genetic inheritance and can disclose vital information about mentality and health. The third step assesses the lines. These are personal signatures and represent an individual's physical, mental, and emotional nature. Events past and present, as well as possible future trends, are all registered here. The life line, head line, and fate line can all be measured, and significant events can be timed with surprising accuracy.

Finally, the fourth step draws together the specific clues that throw light on the particular aspect in question. An analyst who is asked to address a career-related query, for example, might gather in-depth information from the head line, look for confirmation of job

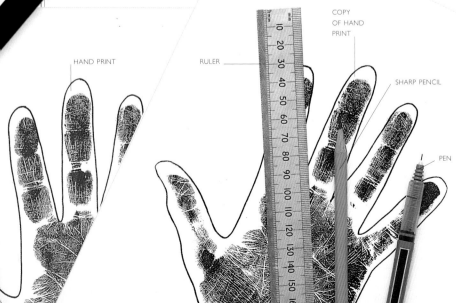

MAGNIFYING GLASS

HAND PRINT

RULER

COPY OF HAND PRINT

SHARP PENCIL

PEN

ESSENTIAL EQUIPMENT
A printing kit and a magnifying glass are essential to the hand reader's art. Taking a print is an important part of consultation, because handprints often highlight markings that may be missed with the naked eye, and a magnifying glass is an invaluable tool for picking out palmar markings during the investigative procedure.

FREEDOM OF CHOICE

CONTRARY TO popular opinion, your fate is not irrevocably engraved in your hands. The lines in your palms can change, sometimes rapidly, in response to a crisis, at other times barely perceptibly. Changes in your lifestyle or your environment will also affect your lines. Hand analysis can show you the possibilities and opportunities that are likely to happen in the future. Whether you choose to develop what is offered or whether you simply ignore the signs, is up to you. Hand analysis demonstrates that your fate is always in your own hands.

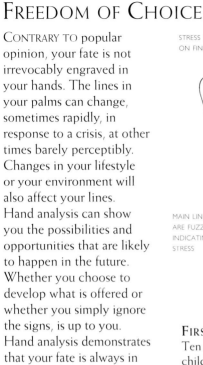

STRESS MARKINGS ON FINGERTIPS

MAIN LINES ARE FUZZY, INDICATING STRESS

PROFUSION OF TINY LINES

FIRST HANDPRINT
Ten months after the birth of her second child, this woman's hand is filled with lines, warning of mental and physical exhaustion.

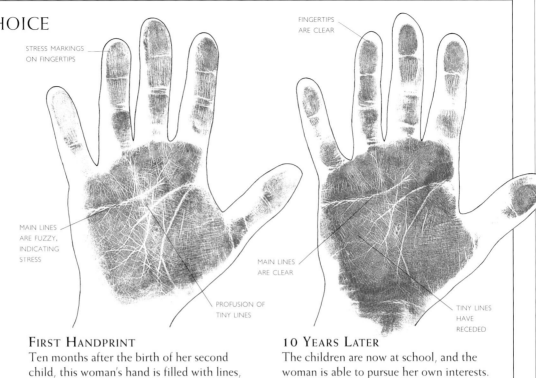

FINGERTIPS ARE CLEAR

MAIN LINES ARE CLEAR

TINY LINES HAVE RECEDED

10 YEARS LATER
The children are now at school, and the woman is able to pursue her own interests. Notice how "calm" the hand has become.

changes on the fate line, and pick out isolated markings associated with individual occupations. Information on every aspect of our lives may be collected and put together in this way.

The Responsible Analyst

Hand analysis is a powerful tool. Those who use it must be aware that seeds of suggestion are easily sown. The wrong deduction, or even a casual comment about a possible event, may have far-reaching consequences, even for a staunch cynic who may chance to reflect upon the remark at a more vulnerable moment in life. It is vitally important, therefore, to give accurate information, and to be aware of self-fulfilling prophecies. It is important to explain about free will – that with positive action it is possible to change not only your destiny, but the lines in your hand. Encouragement should always be given to turn any negative qualities or events into favorable attributes and positive actions.

WHAT CAN ANALYSIS DO?
An analysis of your hands brings to light the intricate patterns that the future holds in store. It also highlights events in your past that may be having repercussions in your life now. Hand analysis enables you to steer around potential problems, grab opportunities, and make the right decisions. In short, an analysis of your hand can help you to take control of your life.

RELATIONSHIPS

P SYCHOLOGISTS AND COUNSELORS would probably agree that forming relationships is one of the most complex of human activities. We are gregarious, and relating is a fundamental aspect of our nature. Many and varied are the relationships that we form in a lifetime, with parents and offspring, friends and colleagues, lovers and partners. Some relationships turn out to be spectacularly successful; others are unmitigated disasters. Whether we triumph or fail largely depends on our disposition and emotional makeup, and these characteristics are mirrored in our hands.

THE FOUR HAND SHAPES

THE FIRST CLUES in putting together a profile of how we relate to others can be found in the basic shape and construction of our hands. The four basic hand shapes reflect our fundamental emotions and reactions, provide a glimpse of how we present ourselves to others, and reveal our emotional potential.

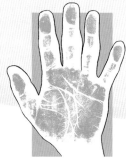

THE EARTH HAND
Known for their honesty and common sense, Earth-handed people tend to be perceived as sincere. They are not deeply romantic or verbally demonstrative but they can be counted on for their loyalty and unfailing support.

THE AIR HAND
Intelligent and witty, the Air hand will have a wide circle of friends, but is highly selective when choosing intimate partners. These people are emotionally stable, but may seem cool and unfriendly. Infidelity can be a problem.

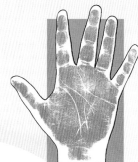

THE FIRE HAND
Fire-handed people travel from misery to elation in a matter of moments. They are warm and caring friends but need lots of reassurance and ego boosting. They fall in and out of love easily, but once settled become constant and ardent lovers.

THE WATER HAND
Caring and compassionate but also sensitive and romantic, Water-handed people are idealistic about their relationships. They are impressionable, and their gentleness may be exploited by more ruthless types.

THE TRIALS OF LOVE

This subject's percussion bows considerably, giving his palm a wide appearance. However, despite the bowed edge, the palm is rectangular and contains a number of strong lines. This suggests the Fire shape, and the whorl fingerprints, which are commonly found on Fire hands, confirm this classification. Fire-handed people fall deeply in love very easily, as a series of relationship lines appearing in his hand testifies. The large island on his head line reveals the unsettling effects of these relationship problems. Luckily, the island ends toward his late 30s, which, coupled with the development of his Apollo line at the same time, suggests that he will soon find his soul mate.

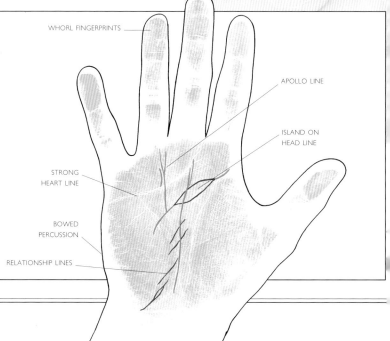

WHORL FINGERPRINTS

APOLLO LINE

ISLAND ON HEAD LINE

STRONG HEART LINE

BOWED PERCUSSION

RELATIONSHIP LINES

EMOTIONAL RESPONSIVENESS

HOW WE RESPOND TO OTHERS, our sexual energy, and our capacity to love are reflected by the overall feel and appearance of the hand. As a general rule, hands that are soft and flabby reveal self-centeredness and self-indulgence. The firmer and harder the hand feels, the more controlled and unyielding the nature will be.

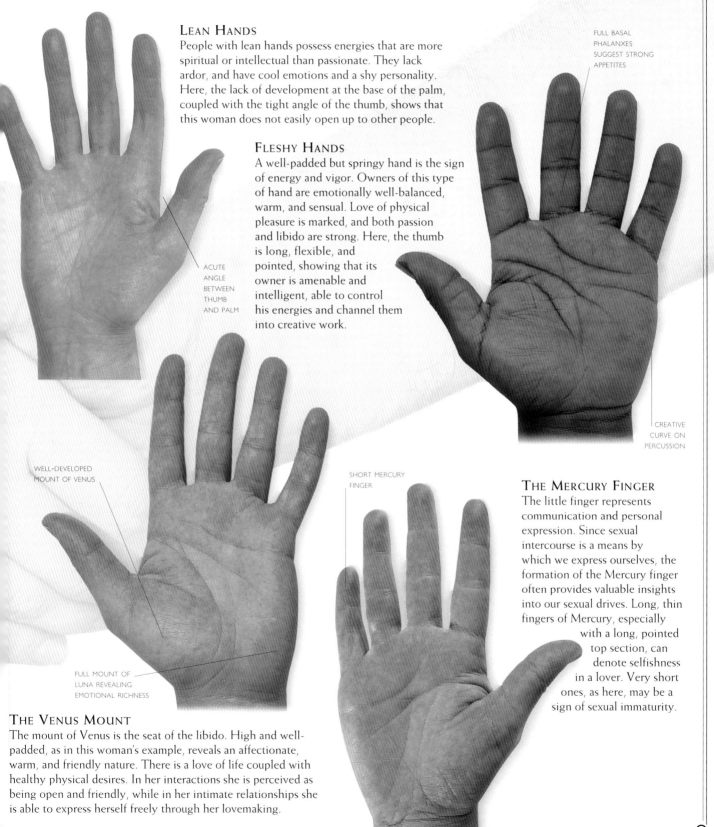

LEAN HANDS
People with lean hands possess energies that are more spiritual or intellectual than passionate. They lack ardor, and have cool emotions and a shy personality. Here, the lack of development at the base of the palm, coupled with the tight angle of the thumb, shows that this woman does not easily open up to other people.

ACUTE ANGLE BETWEEN THUMB AND PALM

FLESHY HANDS
A well-padded but springy hand is the sign of energy and vigor. Owners of this type of hand are emotionally well-balanced, warm, and sensual. Love of physical pleasure is marked, and both passion and libido are strong. Here, the thumb is long, flexible, and pointed, showing that its owner is amenable and intelligent, able to control his energies and channel them into creative work.

FULL BASAL PHALANXES SUGGEST STRONG APPETITES

CREATIVE CURVE ON PERCUSSION

WELL-DEVELOPED MOUNT OF VENUS

FULL MOUNT OF LUNA REVEALING EMOTIONAL RICHNESS

SHORT MERCURY FINGER

THE MERCURY FINGER
The little finger represents communication and personal expression. Since sexual intercourse is a means by which we express ourselves, the formation of the Mercury finger often provides valuable insights into our sexual drives. Long, thin fingers of Mercury, especially with a long, pointed top section, can denote selfishness in a lover. Very short ones, as here, may be a sign of sexual immaturity.

THE VENUS MOUNT
The mount of Venus is the seat of the libido. High and well-padded, as in this woman's example, reveals an affectionate, warm, and friendly nature. There is a love of life coupled with healthy physical desires. In her interactions she is perceived as being open and friendly, while in her intimate relationships she is able to express herself freely through her lovemaking.

RELATIONSHIPS IN THE LINES

To succeed in our relationships we need some degree of self-awareness, and the ability to recognize our emotional patterns, our intimate needs, and motivations. It is only through understanding ourselves that we can begin to really understand others. Since our heart line reflects our feelings and sexual drives, this is the first place we should look (*see page 66*). Other lines in our hands also have some bearing on our relationships. The head line, for example, provides us with insights into our attitudes to others and our emotional expectations.

Analyzing our hands can help to provide the key to understanding the link between our hearts and our heads, but there is even more that our hands can reveal if we know where to look. We all possess particular lines and markings, which not only pinpoint specific relationships but also accurately date when those influences are likely to make their presence felt in our lives.

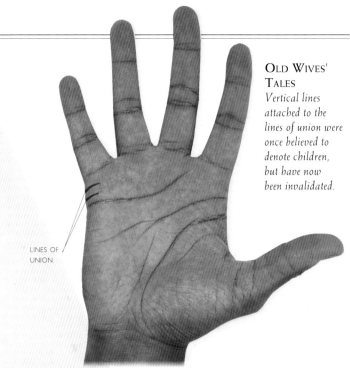

OLD WIVES' TALES
Vertical lines attached to the lines of union were once believed to denote children, but have now been invalidated.

LINES OF UNION

LINES OF UNION
In the past, hand-reading books stated that the small dashes across the percussion edge beneath the Mercury finger represented marriages or love affairs. Consequently, they have been named lines of union or marriage lines. However, after much research, modern analysts doubt these markings are reliable indicators of marriage.

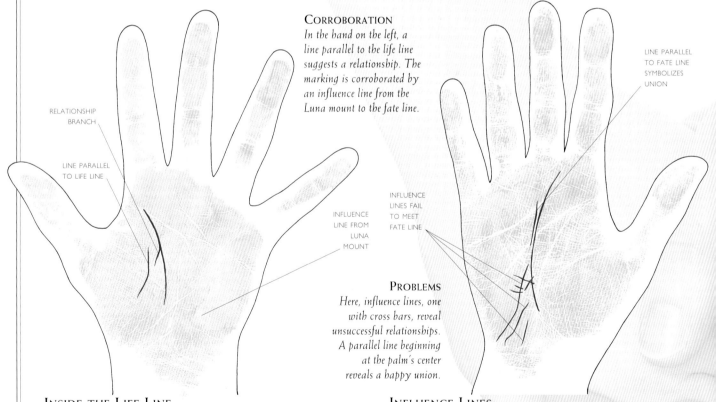

CORROBORATION
In the hand on the left, a line parallel to the life line suggests a relationship. The marking is corroborated by an influence line from the Luna mount to the fate line.

RELATIONSHIP BRANCH

LINE PARALLEL TO LIFE LINE

INFLUENCE LINE FROM LUNA MOUNT

LINE PARALLEL TO FATE LINE SYMBOLIZES UNION

INFLUENCE LINES FAIL TO MEET FATE LINE

PROBLEMS
Here, influence lines, one with cross bars, reveal unsuccessful relationships. A parallel line beginning at the palm's center reveals a happy union.

INSIDE THE LIFE LINE
Look at the inside of the life line for markings that denote relationships. A line parallel to the life line is a sign of a soul mate. Other relationship indicators are branches that appear on the inside of the life line. Depending on age, these branches may mark the beginning of a relationship or the birth of a child.

INFLUENCE LINES
Lines of influence representing relationships sweep up from the Luna area toward the fate line. The success of relationships may be gauged by these lines. Unsuccessful affairs are shown by lines that cut across or fail to meet the fate line, and lines that merge into or run parallel with the fate line symbolize successful unions.

Hennaed Hands

IN INDIA, A BRIDE'S HANDS ARE PAINTED WITH HENNA.

IN A TRADITIONAL Sikh or Hindu marriage it is the custom to paint intricate designs traced in henna over the bride's palms, wrists, and backs of her hands. Part of the ritual of the marriage ceremony involves the bride's hands being studied by the bridegroom. Concealed within the elaborate patterns will be his name, which he must find to ensure that their marriage will be blessed with luck and happiness.

GOOD LUCK
To bring good fortune to the marriage, the bride's female friends and relations also adorn their hands with henna.

TIMING RELATIONSHIPS

IT IS POSSIBLE TO TIME the start and the end of a relationship by applying the timing gauges for the life and fate lines (*see pages 58 and 74*) to the influence lines and relationship branches. This woman's hand reveals that a long relationship failed at age 34. Evidence of a new, more promising relationship begins at age 39.

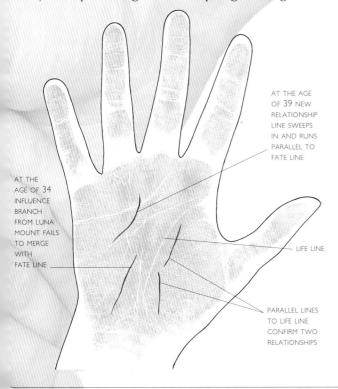

AT THE AGE OF 39 NEW RELATIONSHIP LINE SWEEPS IN AND RUNS PARALLEL TO FATE LINE

AT THE AGE OF 34 INFLUENCE BRANCH FROM LUNA MOUNT FAILS TO MERGE WITH FATE LINE

LIFE LINE

PARALLEL LINES TO LIFE LINE CONFIRM TWO RELATIONSHIPS

LOVE'S HIGHS AND LOWS

OUR HANDS REGISTER the negative and positive events that happen in our lives. In the same way that we can pick out signs of happy, successful unions, we can also spot the problem areas of discord and disunity, and be alert to periods in our lives when we are likely to encounter difficulties in our relationships.

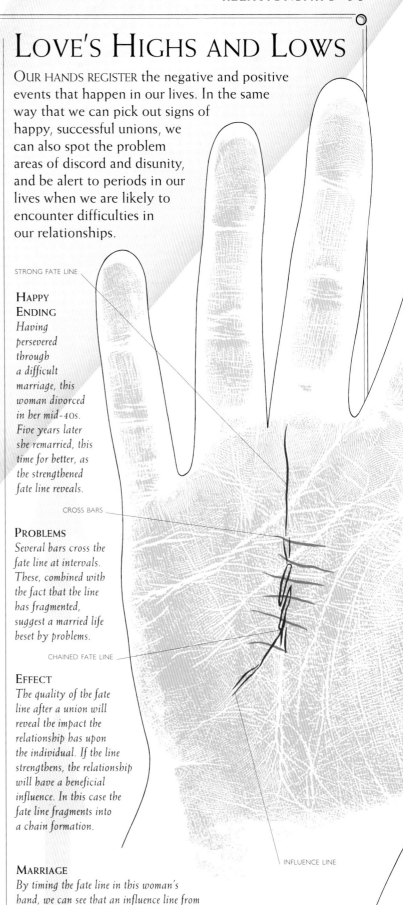

STRONG FATE LINE

HAPPY ENDING
Having persevered through a difficult marriage, this woman divorced in her mid-40s. Five years later she remarried, this time for better, as the strengthened fate line reveals.

CROSS BARS

PROBLEMS
Several bars cross the fate line at intervals. These, combined with the fact that the line has fragmented, suggest a married life beset by problems.

CHAINED FATE LINE

EFFECT
The quality of the fate line after a union will reveal the impact the relationship has upon the individual. If the line strengthens, the relationship will have a beneficial influence. In this case the fate line fragments into a chain formation.

INFLUENCE LINE

MARRIAGE
By timing the fate line in this woman's hand, we can see that an influence line from the Luna mount unites with the fate line, representing her marriage at the age of 32.

COMPATIBILITY

H OW WELL DO YOU get along with your partner? Are you truly compatible? You can answer these questions by comparing your hands. Examining the shapes, structures, and lines of the hands will reveal any differences and similarities and give you insights into your relationship. If there are many similarities it will confirm your compatibility, but, if your hands differ, perhaps pointing out the differences will give you a better understanding of each other. Sometimes it is the differences, not the similarities, that draw two people together.

THE FOUR HAND SHAPES

WHEN LOOKING AT HANDS for signs of compatibility, consider first whether the basic shapes of the hands are in harmony or in conflict with each other. The chart below will reveal your compatibility with other hand shapes. Read your own hand from the horizontal axis, and your partner's from the vertical axis.

	EARTH HAND	AIR HAND	FIRE HAND	WATER HAND	
EARTH HAND	A well-matched combination because both partners are hardworking and soon establish a routine together. A conventional and solid relationship.	A difficult pairing of people with different approaches to life and conflicting attitudes to work. Earth finds the Air partner superficial and lacking in commitment.	A potentially productive partnership. Earth could profit from Fire's enthusiasm. Both have similar energy levels but Fire's wild life-style might irritate Earth.	The least compatible pairing. Water can bring refinement to the relationship, but Earth is infuriated by Water's illogical thinking.	**EARTH HAND**
AIR HAND	Verbally expressive Air finds Earth too quiet. Air requires variety and Earth needs routine. A couple at odds, but each could learn from the other.	A cool, intellectual relationship. Passion and emotion are controlled, and creativity is channeled into ideas. Neither is troubled by sexual jealousy.	A stirring relationship. Both are lively and people-oriented, but different needs could undermine the partnership. Fire's jealousy will make Air feel trapped.	A good combination for a creative partnership. Air could profit from the Water partner's inspired vision. The only snag for Air is that Water can be too possessive.	**AIR HAND**
FIRE HAND	Earth could stabilize Fire's volatility and help to channel ideas constructively. If Fire can stem impatience, this partnership could be mutually rewarding.	With compromise, this could be a mutually satisfying union. Fire must give the Air partner freedom and Air must give physical reassurance in return.	A stimulating, roller-coaster of a relationship, characterized by grand passion. To keep the flame lit, each must respect the other's need for attention.	A good combination. Both are passionate, and together they produce a steamy and sultry relationship. Fire will enjoy being allowed to take the lead.	**FIRE HAND**
WATER HAND	A difficult union between very different people. Positively, Earth could help to materialize Water's dreams. Negatively, Water finds Earth insensitive.	A shared creative approach to life, where Air could provide the worldliness Water requires. Sometimes, the Water partner can find Air too emotionally distant.	This relationship is highly promising. Both enjoy plenty of affection and displays of emotion. Water benefits especially from Fire's worldliness.	A meeting of souls characterizes this refined couple, who live for their art. Joint idealism, however, suggests little understanding of worldly life.	**WATER HAND**

COMPATIBILITY BETWEEN LINES

COMPARING AND CONTRASTING the hand shapes is the first level of analysis when considering compatibility between two people. The next stage is to add any information gleaned from an analysis of the head, life, and heart lines. This may overcome any differences that were highlighted between the hand shapes.

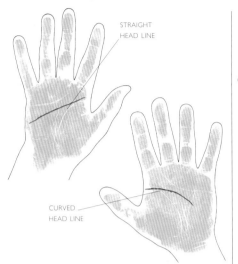

STRAIGHT HEAD LINE

CURVED HEAD LINE

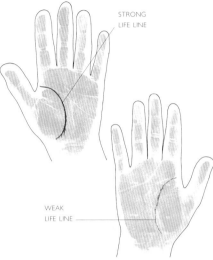

STRONG LIFE LINE

WEAK LIFE LINE

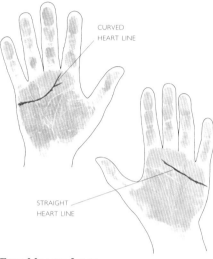

CURVED HEART LINE

STRAIGHT HEART LINE

THE HEAD LINE

For the basic distinctions between a straight head line and a curved one, see page 62. If both partners have straight head lines, they take a practical approach to life. When both partners have curved head lines, they both see life on a broader canvas. With dissimilar head lines, interests and attitudes will differ. People with different head lines may be complementary but there is little meeting of minds.

THE LIFE LINE

When comparing life lines, consider their construction and course. A chained life line on one hand, for example, shows low energy levels, while a strong life line in the partner's hand reveals robust good health. A life line that sweeps wide around the mount of Venus, indicator of libido and sexual energy, denotes a passionate person, but a life line that is tight to the thumb points to a low sex drive (*see page 54*).

THE HEART LINE

Well-matched heart lines, in terms of length and direction of travel, show that partners understand each other's moods. The difference between the straight and curved heart line is that the former implies rational feelings while the latter reveals emotional responses (*see page 67*). However, complementary emotions, one rational, for example, and the other emotional, may contribute to a strong relationship.

CASE HISTORY

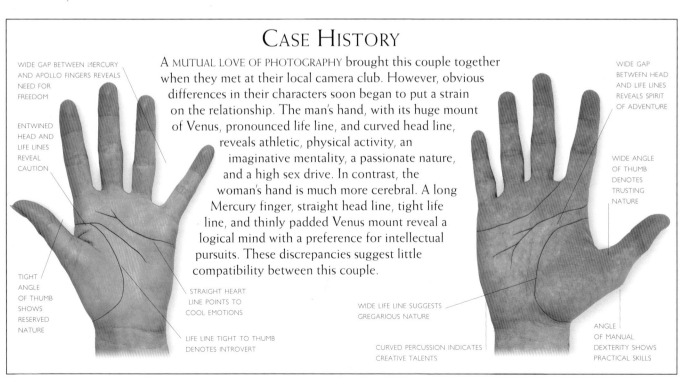

A MUTUAL LOVE OF PHOTOGRAPHY brought this couple together when they met at their local camera club. However, obvious differences in their characters soon began to put a strain on the relationship. The man's hand, with its huge mount of Venus, pronounced life line, and curved head line, reveals athletic, physical activity, an imaginative mentality, a passionate nature, and a high sex drive. In contrast, the woman's hand is much more cerebral. A long Mercury finger, straight head line, tight life line, and thinly padded Venus mount reveal a logical mind with a preference for intellectual pursuits. These discrepancies suggest little compatibility between this couple.

WIDE GAP BETWEEN MERCURY AND APOLLO FINGERS REVEALS NEED FOR FREEDOM

ENTWINED HEAD AND LIFE LINES REVEAL CAUTION

TIGHT ANGLE OF THUMB SHOWS RESERVED NATURE

STRAIGHT HEART LINE POINTS TO COOL EMOTIONS

LIFE LINE TIGHT TO THUMB DENOTES INTROVERT

WIDE GAP BETWEEN HEAD AND LIFE LINES REVEALS SPIRIT OF ADVENTURE

WIDE ANGLE OF THUMB DENOTES TRUSTING NATURE

WIDE LIFE LINE SUGGESTS GREGARIOUS NATURE

CURVED PERCUSSION INDICATES CREATIVE TALENTS

ANGLE OF MANUAL DEXTERITY SHOWS PRACTICAL SKILLS

THE FAMILY

WHICH PLAYS THE GREATER role in shaping our behavioral development, heredity factors or environmental conditioning? Analyzing the hands of family groups suggests that both are influential. Certainly, similar characteristics are passed down from one generation to another, because the hand shape, fingerprints, and other specific markings recur within families. However, lines change, discrepancies occur between the hands, and markings reveal predisposition rather than irrevocable outcome. Together, these factors suggest that we are in charge of our own destiny.

APPLYING HAND ANALYSIS TO A FAMILY

FAMILIES ARE MADE UP of complex networks of relationships – some members get along better together than others, some resemble one another, and some turn out to be black sheep, not fitting in anywhere. Comparing the hands of a family may, at least in part, explain the reasons why.

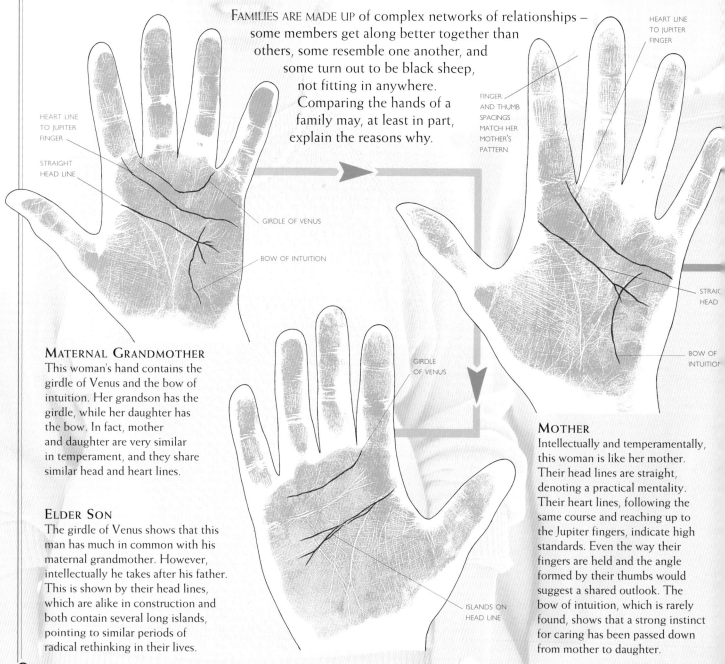

HEART LINE
TO JUPITER
FINGER

STRAIGHT
HEAD LINE

GIRDLE OF VENUS

BOW OF INTUITION

HEART LINE
TO JUPITER
FINGER

FINGER
AND THUMB
SPACINGS
MATCH HER
MOTHER'S
PATTERN

STRAIG
HEAD

BOW OF
INTUITION

GIRDLE
OF VENUS

ISLANDS ON
HEAD LINE

MATERNAL GRANDMOTHER
This woman's hand contains the girdle of Venus and the bow of intuition. Her grandson has the girdle, while her daughter has the bow. In fact, mother and daughter are very similar in temperament, and they share similar head and heart lines.

ELDER SON
The girdle of Venus shows that this man has much in common with his maternal grandmother. However, intellectually he takes after his father. This is shown by their head lines, which are alike in construction and both contain several long islands, pointing to similar periods of radical rethinking in their lives.

MOTHER
Intellectually and temperamentally, this woman is like her mother. Their head lines are straight, denoting a practical mentality. Their heart lines, following the same course and reaching up to the Jupiter fingers, indicate high standards. Even the way their fingers are held and the angle formed by their thumbs would suggest a shared outlook. The bow of intuition, which is rarely found, shows that a strong instinct for caring has been passed down from mother to daughter.

The Genetic Inheritance of the Hand

IT IS OUR CHROMOSOMAL BLUEPRINT THAT GOVERNS
THE TYPE OF HAND WE INHERIT.

IN THE SAME WAY THAT our genes determine the color of
our eyes, or decree whether we will be tall or short, our
chromosomal blueprints are responsible for the shape of
our hands, for the skin ridge patterns that are stamped into
our skin, and even for the types of lines that cross our palms.
Our pattern of inheritance is nowhere more evident than
in our fingerprint patterns, which may be traced through
a family from one member to another.

FAMILY TREE
*Using our handprints, we
can build up a family tree.
Characteristic markings
and similarities can be
traced in the shape and
construction of the hands
of the family members.*

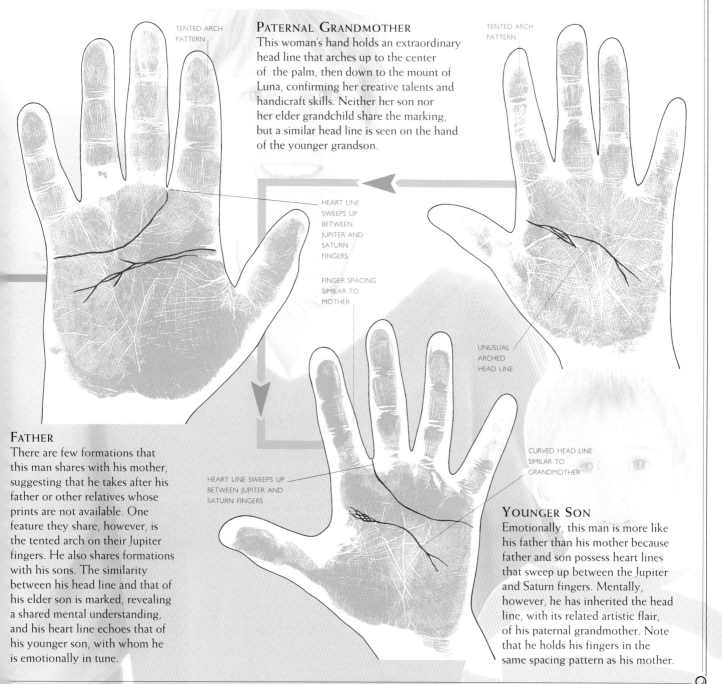

TENTED ARCH
PATTERN

PATERNAL GRANDMOTHER
This woman's hand holds an extraordinary
head line that arches up to the center
of the palm, then down to the mount of
Luna, confirming her creative talents and
handicraft skills. Neither her son nor
her elder grandchild share the marking,
but a similar head line is seen on the hand
of the younger grandson.

TENTED ARCH
PATTERN

HEART LINE
SWEEPS UP
BETWEEN
JUPITER AND
SATURN
FINGERS

FINGER SPACING
SIMILAR TO
MOTHER

UNUSUAL
ARCHED
HEAD LINE

FATHER
There are few formations that
this man shares with his mother,
suggesting that he takes after his
father or other relatives whose
prints are not available. One
feature they share, however, is
the tented arch on their Jupiter
fingers. He also shares formations
with his sons. The similarity
between his head line and that of
his elder son is marked, revealing
a shared mental understanding,
and his heart line echoes that of
his younger son, with whom he
is emotionally in tune.

HEART LINE SWEEPS UP
BETWEEN JUPITER AND
SATURN FINGERS

CURVED HEAD LINE
SIMILAR TO
GRANDMOTHER

YOUNGER SON
Emotionally, this man is more like
his father than his mother because
father and son possess heart lines
that sweep up between the Jupiter
and Saturn fingers. Mentally,
however, he has inherited the head
line, with its related artistic flair,
of his paternal grandmother. Note
that he holds his fingers in the
same spacing pattern as his mother.

OCCUPATIONS

H AND READING can be useful when seeking an appropriate career because our hands reflect our mental aptitude and innate talents. Assessing your suitability for a particular type of job requires you to pick out the relevant clues and build up your information, level by level.

This will take you from broad generalizations, seen in the shape and construction of your hand, to specific details, pinpointed by your lines and special markings. Sifting through the data will give you a clear view of the sort of occupation that will bring you job satisfaction and success.

THE FOUR HAND SHAPES

THE GENERAL SHAPE OF our hands outlines our basic nature, and provides the first clues to the broad occupational areas that would suit our inherent talents and skills. Later, we can build on this, adding information that we glean from our fingerprints or lines in order to define the categories further.

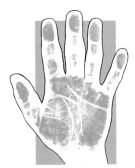

THE EARTH HAND
Earth-handed people are best suited to outdoor occupations and are industrious workers. Good with their hands, what they may lack in imagination they make up for in practical skills. They hate change and need job security.

THE AIR HAND
Communication is the forte of Air-handed people, and they prefer working in education, the media, sales, the travel industry, and politics. They are whiz-kids with machinery, computers, electronics, and all manner of modern gadgetry.

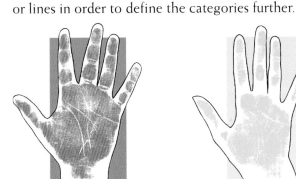

THE FIRE HAND
Leaders and organizers, Fire-handed people like to control situations. People-oriented, they gravitate toward the world of entertainment and performing arts. They thrive on challenge and adventure and work well under stress.

THE WATER HAND
Two distinct areas appeal to the Water hand: the caring professions and the arts. They make excellent therapists, both in the traditional and holistic fields, but they are equally happy as artists, poets, and designers.

Hands in Competition

HAND SHAPES CONFIRM THAT DIFFERENT JOBS DEMAND UNIQUE SKILLS.

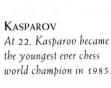

COMPARE THE HANDS of Gary Kasparov and Muhammad Ali. Both are contestants in one-to-one duels that require calculative skills and fast reactions, but each needs to respond on a different level. Kasparov's lean hands and knotty fingers reveal the capacity for intellectual reasoning and quick responses. Ali's hand shows meaty development at the base, the repository of stamina and instinctive reactions.

KASPAROV
At 22, Kasparov became the youngest ever chess world champion in 1985.

ALI
Muhammad Ali won the world heavyweight boxing championship three times.

THE MOUNTS

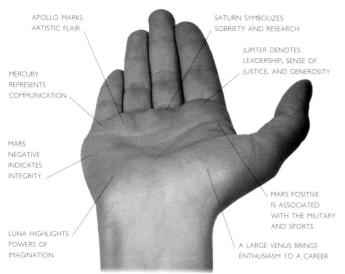

APOLLO MARKS
ARTISTIC FLAIR

SATURN SYMBOLIZES
SOBRIETY AND RESEARCH

JUPITER DENOTES
LEADERSHIP, SENSE OF
JUSTICE, AND GENEROSITY

MERCURY
REPRESENTS
COMMUNICATION

MARS
NEGATIVE
INDICATES
INTEGRITY

MARS POSITIVE
IS ASSOCIATED
WITH THE MILITARY
AND SPORTS

LUNA HIGHLIGHTS
POWERS OF
IMAGINATION

A LARGE VENUS BRINGS
ENTHUSIASM TO A CAREER

THE MOUNTS REPRESENT the storehouses of our energies and can pinpoint where our talents lie. In general, a high mount indicates discriminative powers and expertise. One that is widespread shows plenty of talent but it is unchanneled. A mount that is flat denotes poorly developed interests in that area.

FINGERPRINT PATTERNS

OUR FINGERPRINT PATTERNS are inherited and show our genetic disposition. With education and training we can modify or develop our personalities, but our fingerprints will always reveal our basic instincts.

LOOPS
People with loops are best suited to teamwork, in an environment that provides variety and stimulation.

COMPOSITES
Good at seeing both sides of the picture, these people make excellent negotiators, counselors, and judges.

WHORLS
The mark of the expert and the specialist. Better working alone rather than as part of a team, they need to be in control of their environment.

ARCHES
From artisan to engineer and farmer to surgeon, the very practical owners of the arch excel in occupations that require manual skill.

THE FINGERS

OUR FINGERS INDICATE how we direct our skills. They reveal how we handle our tasks, undertake our duties, and carry out the requirements of the job.

FINGER LENGTH

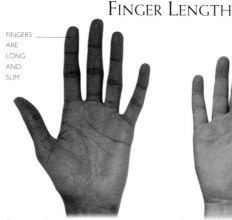

FINGERS
ARE
LONG
AND
SLIM

FINGERS
ARE
SHORT
AND
THICK

LONG FINGERS
Owners of long fingers have a genius for dealing with detail. Careful and painstaking, they are best suited to occupations that demand a meticulous or analytical mentality. They particularly excel at tasks requiring precision and good hand-eye coordination. However, being so thorough means they are also slow.

SHORT FINGERS
Possessing short fingers indicates the ability to process information rapidly. Often inspired thinkers, their owners feel their way through a task intuitively, seeing the overall plan on a large scale. They are excellent planners but lack patience and have a tendency to take any shortcut that will bring them to their objective.

FINGER JOINTS

PRONOUNCED
JOINTS

SMOOTH
JOINTS

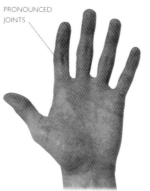

PRONOUNCED JOINTS
Pronounced joints are the mark of the analyst. Owners excel at digging out facts and assessing information. They are problem-solvers and are often drawn to occupations that require a logical mind. Suitable careers might include science, research, philosophy, debate, or any other area where a reasoned approach is required.

SMOOTH JOINTS
People with smooth joints tend to assimilate information intuitively. Rather than reasoning through a problem, they prefer to follow their instincts. Tasks requiring the ability to make fast assessments are suited to these types. They work well with others and gravitate toward creative occupations.

OCCUPATIONS IN THE LINES

HAVING RECOGNIZED THE general occupational areas to which you are suited according to the construction of your hand, you can now begin to fill out the picture by adding clues gathered from your major lines. These lines show your particular mental aptitude and can even reveal when you are next likely to change your job.

THE APOLLO LINE

FINANCIAL NECESSITY and the lack of training or opportunity often means that we have to make do with a job that fails to exercise our innate talent. How we fare under such circumstances is revealed by the Apollo line.

MULTIPLE APOLLO LINES

SINGLE APOLLO LINE
The Apollo line is an indicator of job satisfaction. When it is strong, it denotes that we feel happy and fulfilled and that, whatever occupation we are pursuing, we are receiving due acknowledgment and reward for our work.

SINGLE APOLLO LINE

MULTIPLE APOLLO LINES
Multiple Apollo lines reveal a multitalented individual – someone who has the ability, and the need, to juggle several disparate jobs or tasks at the same time. Perhaps this is a sign of a low boredom threshold, or perhaps it denotes such mental dexterity that the attention can happily be divided between different interests. Multiple Apollo lines belong to flexible, adaptable workers who would positively welcome and enjoy several career changes.

THE HEAD LINE

ONCE YOU HAVE ESTABLISHED the requirements of a job, one of the best ways to determine your aptitude and mental suitability for that line of work is to look at your head line. This line reveals how you think, and describes your mentality and intellectual ability. Parents and career advisors would do well to consider the head line when offering guidance on suitable employment.

A CURVED HEAD LINE
There are two basic forms of the head line that distinguish an aptitude for scientific subjects from a flair for creative thinking. A curved head line denotes an ability to think widely and laterally. It is found in the hands of people who enjoy working in the arts and humanities. Competent communicators, they are drawn to occupations in the media, advertising, public relations, and art and design.

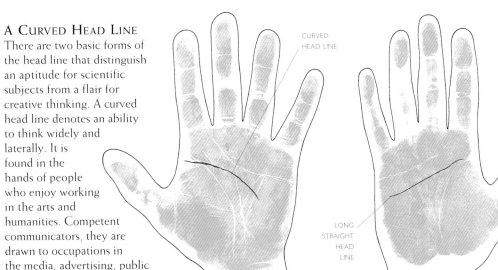

CURVED HEAD LINE

LONG STRAIGHT HEAD LINE

A STRAIGHT HEAD LINE
The straight head line is a mark of the person who takes a logical, analytical approach to life. These people gravitate toward the scientific, mathematical, technological, or business-oriented professions. Very long head lines reveal an ability to focus on the task in hand, often signifying academic achievement. Short, straight head lines highlight a practical mentality with interests of a more materialistic nature.

THE FATE LINE

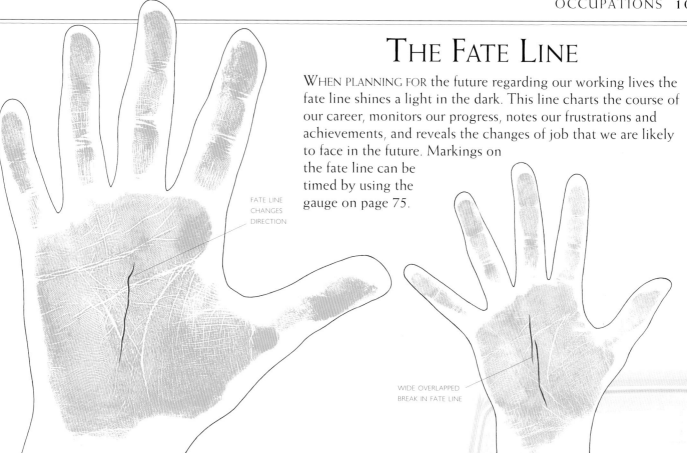

WHEN PLANNING FOR the future regarding our working lives the fate line shines a light in the dark. This line charts the course of our career, monitors our progress, notes our frustrations and achievements, and reveals the changes of job that we are likely to face in the future. Markings on the fate line can be timed by using the gauge on page 75.

FATE LINE CHANGES DIRECTION

WIDE OVERLAPPED BREAK IN FATE LINE

THE FATE LINE CHANGES DIRECTION

When the fate line changes direction along its route, a change is in store. However, because there is no break in the line, it is unlikely to denote a new career or even a job with a different company. Confirming that the links with the employment are kept, the deviation is likely to indicate a new orientation, or, as with the owner of this handprint, a promotion within the same company.

A WIDE OVERLAPPED BREAK

Change is denoted by a break in the fate line, but note that there are two distinct types of breaks. In this case, the break occurs with overlapped ends, which reveals that the individual herself made the decision to change jobs. The width of the gap shows the extent of the change. Here, the gap is wide, reflecting that she has radically changed careers and moved to a different part of the country.

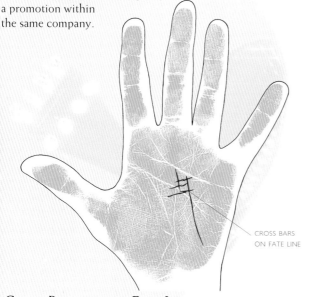

CROSS BARS ON FATE LINE

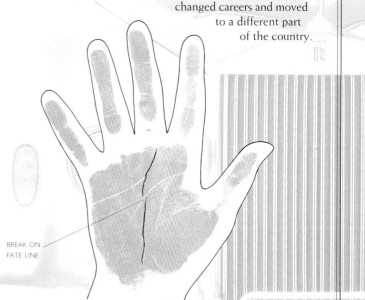

BREAK ON FATE LINE

CROSS BARS ON THE FATE LINE

A cross bar on the fate line warns of obstacles. Personal worries or a personality clash with a superior may affect one's work. In this woman's case, a colleague blocked her progress. The consequent broken fate line shows that she chose to change her job, and the strength of the new line reveals that it was a positive move.

A COMPLETE BREAK IN THE FATE LINE

While an overlapped break reveals change that has been planned and instigated by its owner, the complete break denotes an enforced change, an event outside the owner's control. Perhaps this might be due to a medical condition forcing the individual to give up work or, as in this case, being laid off from work.

PROFESSIONS IN THE PALMS

EACH JOB HAS A DEFINED set of requirements – accountancy, for example, demands numeracy, and fashion design calls for artistic flair. An accomplished mathematician, though possibly able to design a show-stopping Paris collection, is more likely to find success on the floor of the stock exchange than in a house of haute couture. Similarly, the fashion designer may be efficient at keeping the company's accounts, but might find creative inspiration stifled working all day in a bank.

It is the aptitude with numbers, or the eye for line and color, that individualizes these examples. These are the kinds of talents that are highlighted in our hands by special markings, pointing out the professions to which we are best suited.

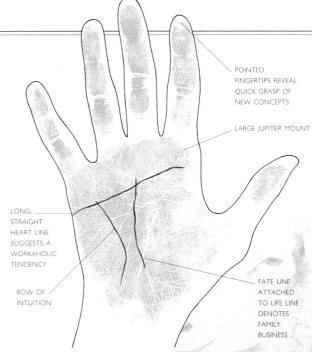

POINTED FINGERTIPS REVEAL QUICK GRASP OF NEW CONCEPTS

LARGE JUPITER MOUNT

LONG, STRAIGHT HEART LINE SUGGESTS A WORKAHOLIC TENDENCY

BOW OF INTUITION

FATE LINE ATTACHED TO LIFE LINE DENOTES FAMILY BUSINESS

COMPANY DIRECTOR
Leadership qualities are highlighted here by a large Jupiter mount. Foresight and the ability to make quick judgments are aided by a finely marked bow of intuition. The pressures that accompany a demanding occupation are reflected in the plethora of lines all over this palm, and in the form of stress markings on the fingertips.

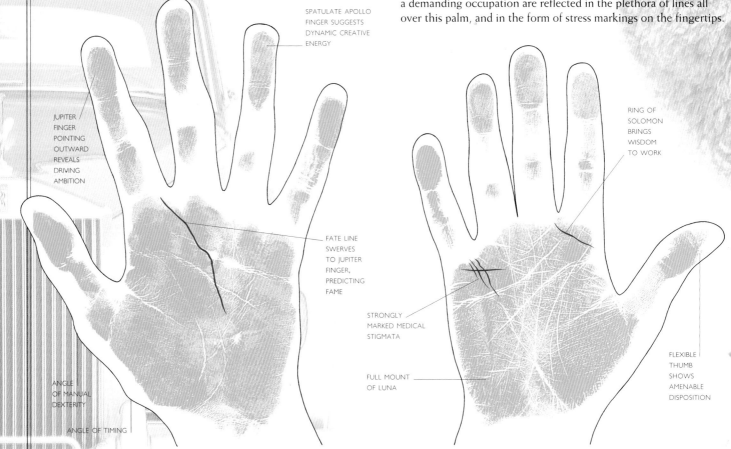

SPATULATE APOLLO FINGER SUGGESTS DYNAMIC CREATIVE ENERGY

JUPITER FINGER POINTING OUTWARD REVEALS DRIVING AMBITION

FATE LINE SWERVES TO JUPITER FINGER, PREDICTING FAME

ANGLE OF MANUAL DEXTERITY

ANGLE OF TIMING

RING OF SOLOMON BRINGS WISDOM TO WORK

STRONGLY MARKED MEDICAL STIGMATA

FULL MOUNT OF LUNA

FLEXIBLE THUMB SHOWS AMENABLE DISPOSITION

MUSICIAN
This violinist has a defined angle of timing at the base of his hand, and the angle of manual dexterity at the base of the thumb ensures nimble fingers. His widely spaced fingers show the passion he puts into his music, but the tight angle of the thumb testifies to the long hours of practice he puts into his work.

NURSE
A natural instinct for healing and a life devoted to caring for others are symbolized here by the medical stigmata, badge of those in the medical professions. Arched fingerprints reveal a no-nonsense approach that inspires confidence in this nurse's patients. The full mount of Luna adds understanding, compassion, and empathy.

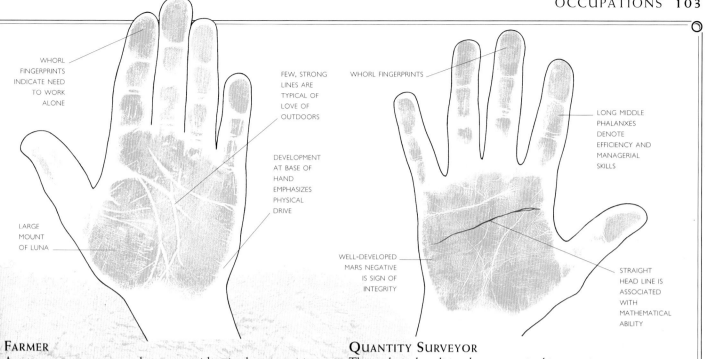

WHORL FINGERPRINTS INDICATE NEED TO WORK ALONE

FEW, STRONG LINES ARE TYPICAL OF LOVE OF OUTDOORS

DEVELOPMENT AT BASE OF HAND EMPHASIZES PHYSICAL DRIVE

LARGE MOUNT OF LUNA

WHORL FINGERPRINTS

LONG MIDDLE PHALANXES DENOTE EFFICIENCY AND MANAGERIAL SKILLS

WELL-DEVELOPED MARS NEGATIVE IS SIGN OF INTEGRITY

STRAIGHT HEAD LINE IS ASSOCIATED WITH MATHEMATICAL ABILITY

FARMER

An attunement to nature and a rapport with animals, prerequisites for a successful career in agriculture, are contained in this farmer's hand. Note the heavy development of the thumb and the base of the hand, which both highlight physical strength, and the large mount of Luna, revealing a sensitivity to the rhythm of the seasons.

QUANTITY SURVEYOR

The analytical qualities that are required in quantity surveying are ably met here by the long, straight head line. Practical know-how is denoted by the square palm and blunt fingers. A full set of whorl fingerprints adds the ability to focus on the task at hand. The strong, well-balanced thumb points to a decisive nature.

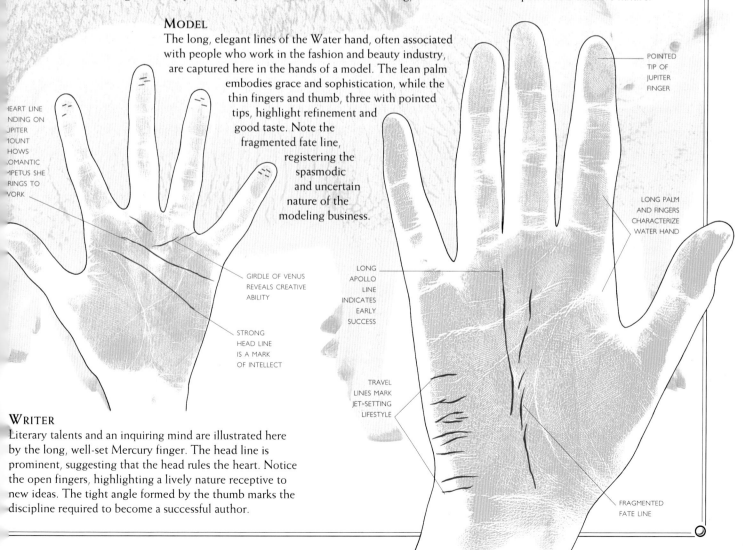

MODEL

The long, elegant lines of the Water hand, often associated with people who work in the fashion and beauty industry, are captured here in the hands of a model. The lean palm embodies grace and sophistication, while the thin fingers and thumb, three with pointed tips, highlight refinement and good taste. Note the fragmented fate line, registering the spasmodic and uncertain nature of the modeling business.

HEART LINE ENDING ON JUPITER MOUNT SHOWS ROMANTIC IMPETUS SHE BRINGS TO WORK

GIRDLE OF VENUS REVEALS CREATIVE ABILITY

STRONG HEAD LINE IS A MARK OF INTELLECT

POINTED TIP OF JUPITER FINGER

LONG PALM AND FINGERS CHARACTERIZE WATER HAND

LONG APOLLO LINE INDICATES EARLY SUCCESS

TRAVEL LINES MARK JET-SETTING LIFESTYLE

FRAGMENTED FATE LINE

WRITER

Literary talents and an inquiring mind are illustrated here by the long, well-set Mercury finger. The head line is prominent, suggesting that the head rules the heart. Notice the open fingers, highlighting a lively nature receptive to new ideas. The tight angle formed by the thumb marks the discipline required to become a successful author.

HEALTH

FOR CENTURIES, PHYSICIANS have recognized a link between the condition of our hands and nails and our health. Modern medical researchers have confirmed this link by showing that certain fingerprint markings are associated with a predisposition to heart disease. This is only the tip of the iceberg, for our hands are registers that provide us with clues about the current state of our health and our susceptibility to disease. It must be stressed, however, that the markings pinpoint a tendency only, and do not imply that a disease will inevitably develop.

THE FOUR HAND SHAPES

PSYCHOLOGISTS HAVE SHOWN that particular groups of people are susceptible to certain diseases. Tense, competitive individuals are more prone to heart disease than calm, relaxed ones. These findings confirm that our personalities affect our health – and our personalities are reflected in our hands.

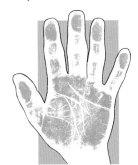

THE EARTH HAND
Susceptible to bowel or intestinal problems due to worry and overindulgence, Earth-handed people need to reduce stress and avoid gaining weight. A good exercise routine with plenty of fresh air is essential for their well-being.

THE AIR HAND
Nervous tension and respiratory problems are typical of Air hands. Their overactive minds make incessant demands on their nervous systems, often leading to exhaustion. They should ensure that they have periods of mental relaxation.

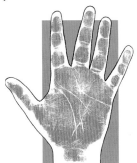

THE FIRE HAND
Dynamic Fire hands are prone to cardiovascular problems. Accidents and injuries can result from their hastiness and impulsive actions. Fire-handed people need to learn to pace themselves; otherwise they can suffer burnout.

THE WATER HAND
A delicate nervous system makes this group prone to psychological problems. Allergies and rheumatic conditions are also common. Water-handed people should avoid a tendency toward addiction to drugs or alcohol.

THE MOUSE

WHEN THE HAND is formed into a fist and the thumb is pressed up against the curled fingers, the muscle behind the thumb humps up to form a hillock known as the "mouse." The firmer the mouse, the stronger the constitution and resistance to disease. A mouse that is soft to the touch suggests lowered vitality. If the muscle shows signs of wasting, it may be an early warning of diabetes.

THE MOUSE

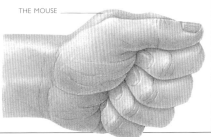

Freckles on the Palm

DO YOU HAVE A FRECKLE ON YOUR PALM?

OCCASIONALLY, on some people's palms, a small brown spot resembling a solitary freckle may be seen. It appears to show through from beneath the layers of skin rather than on the surface of the palm. It is usually found low down on the hand or on the percussion area and is thought to suggest a copper deficiency.

PALM CONSISTENCY

A HEALTHY CONSTITUTION is revealed by good muscle tone in the padding that covers the palm, making the mounts springy to the touch. A hand with this elastic "give," rather like that of a rubber ball, shows a resistance to poor health and an ability to recuperate quickly and easily following a bout of illness.

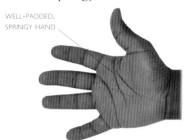

WELL-PADDED, SPRINGY HAND

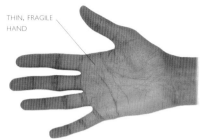

THIN, FRAGILE HAND

HOLLOW PALM

THICK PALM
This man's thick, well-padded but springy hand denotes a robust constitution. A thick palm with soft, doughy mounts reveals a lack of energy and is associated with an imbalance of the thyroid gland. Hard and unyielding, thick palms show insensitivity and emotional repression.

THIN PALM
Thin, fragile hands suggest a delicate constitution with limited stores of energy. This woman's thin hand warns that she lives on her nerves, and when she succumbs to a bout of poor health it may take a long time to recuperate fully and get back on her feet again.

HOLLOW PALM
If the surrounding mounts are well-padded, the palm may appear hollow, especially if the Venus and Luna mounts dominate. When all the mounts are of average size and the palm still appears scooped out, as in this woman's hand, it reveals poor physical reserves and little staying power.

MARKINGS ON THE FINGERTIPS

EACH FINGER IS LINKED to a specific aspect of life or part of the body, therefore fingertip markings can reveal important information about our health. Short, horizontal dashes denote stress, while vertical lines may point to hormonal problems. Both types of markings will disappear with restored health.

HORIZONTAL LINES

VERTICAL LINES
Evidence suggests that a relationship exists between the fingers and the endocrine system. The Jupiter finger is said to be linked with the pituitary gland; therefore, vertical lines on the tip of this finger suggest problems with the action of that gland. Vertical lines on the Saturn finger allude to the function of the pineal gland. The Apollo finger is associated to the thymus gland and vertical lines on this tip may imply problems with the cardiovascular system, pointing to potential irregularities in blood pressure. On the Mercury fingertip, vertical lines are believed to denote faulty action of the thyroid gland.

VERTICAL LINES

HORIZONTAL LINES
When horizontal lines occur across the Jupiter fingertips, they point to a crisis of confidence. On the Saturn finger, they reveal worries about home and security. Horizontal lines across the Apollo finger represent obstacles to happiness. When both the Saturn and Apollo fingers are more heavily scored by horizontal lines than the other digits, the individual's relationship or marriage may be under threat. Horizontal lines on the Mercury fingertip highlight a communication block or sexual problem of some kind.

SKIN PATTERNS AND YOUR HEALTH

THE GENERAL APPEARANCE of the lines and ridge patterns in our palms gives valuable information about our well-being. Signs of wear and tear, warnings of possible problems to come, and predisposition to ailments are detectable before other clinical symptoms appear. By spotting clues in advance it may be possible to take preventive action and devise strategies for good health.

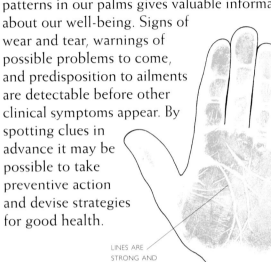

LINES ARE STRONG AND PALM IS CLEAR

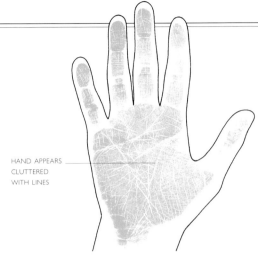

HAND APPEARS CLUTTERED WITH LINES

A FULL HAND

A hand covered in a cobweb of lines is known as a "full" hand. This is a sign that the nervous system is stretched, and/or that its owner is high-strung. The imagination may run out of control, resulting in anxiety and psychosomatic disorders. With stress management and a more relaxed lifestyle, balance can be restored.

AN EMPTY HAND

The "empty" hand contains only the major lines and the palm is uncluttered. Here, the nervous system is balanced and its owner calm and able to take the stresses of life in his or her stride.

IMPAIRED LINES

CLEAR, STRONG LINES in the hand are thought to reflect robust health. It follows that any impairment of the lines reveals that the constitution is somehow weakened. A series of islands or chains in the head or heart lines may point to an imbalance of the biochemistry due to mineral deficiencies. A similar effect on the life line reveals poor vitality and a weakened constitution.

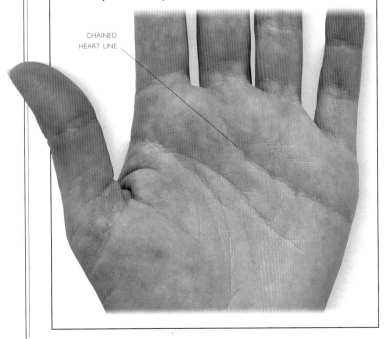

CHAINED HEART LINE

SKIN RIDGES

CONGENITAL ABNORMALITIES such as Down's syndrome are mirrored in skin ridge markings. Scientists have also found other links between skin patterns and disease.

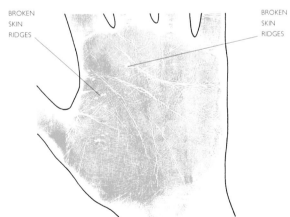

BROKEN SKIN RIDGES

BROKEN SKIN RIDGES

DAMAGED RIDGES

The condition of the skin ridges will give an indication about the general health of both the nervous and immune systems of the individual. This is because the ridges and entire palmar surface of the hand are covered with nerve endings, sending messages and receiving electrical impulses via the nervous and endocrine systems to and from the brain. If those systems are weakened by poor health or overloaded due to neurological disorders, it causes the ridges to break down, almost as if they had been snipped through. Above, the white patches, virtually undetectable with the naked eye, are in fact broken ridge lines following skin cancer and chemotherapy treatment.

HEALTH MARKINGS

IT HAS BEEN OBSERVED that particular markings in our hands are associated with certain medical conditions. Some we inherit and some develop as environmental factors affect our health. All markings, however, only denote potential, predisposition, or possibility. The mere presence of a marking does not imply that a full-blown condition will inevitably develop. Diagnosis should never be based on one feature alone, nor ever pronounced without medical training. But if in any doubt, advice from a physician should be sought.

LADDERED HEART LINE
Sometimes, a patch of the heart line may be seen to stratify into a ladder effect just beneath the Apollo finger. This formation may imply a calcium imbalance and a subsequent disturbance to the normal sleep pattern.

ORTHODONTAL MARKINGS
A group of tiny lines lying just above the heart line, below the Apollo and Mercury fingers, is associated with dental problems. These lines should not be confused with the larger markings, also in this area, of the medical stigmata.

STAR ON THE LINE
A star on a line denotes a sudden impact, physical or psychological. On the heart line, with other corroboration, it may denote the onset of a cardiac problem. On the head line, it may denote a blow to the head. On the life line it points to injury or surgery.

INTESTINAL LINES
A patch of fine lines rising obliquely through the center of the palm suggests a tendency to digestive, gastric, or intestinal disorders.

VEILING
A cluster of fine, superficial crossing lines on the percussion is associated with a buildup of uric acid in the system that could potentially trigger rheumatic conditions.

INDENTATIONS IN THE HEAD LINE
If, when the hand is stretched, a series of tiny indentations as small as pinpricks are seen in the head line, suspect a predisposition to headaches and migraine.

EXTRA-LONG HEAD LINE
A head line that stretches across the palm right to the percussion edge is often a sign of hyperactivity and behavioral problems, especially in youngsters. However, this should not be confused with the Simian line, which combines both head and heart lines in one, and also runs right across the palm.

ALLERGY LINE
Traditionally called the Via Lascivia, the presence of a long line that enters from the percussion edge and lies across the Luna mount points to a general sensitivity to allergens and as such is now called the allergy line.

ISLANDS ON THE HEART LINE
An island occurring on the heart line beneath the Saturn finger is associated with hearing defects, but if one is found on the line beneath the Apollo finger, it points to ophthalmic weaknesses.

DROPPED BRANCH
When a tiny, fine branch drops out of the head line it often coincides with a time of depression. Occasionally, the head line will dip at that point too, recovery taking place as the head line rises again and evens out. The onset and duration of this period can be timed and thus, perhaps, averted.

FUZZY HEAD LINE
If anywhere along its length the head line forms into a wide fluffy patch, it tells of a period of mental strain.

ISLANDS ON THE LIFE LINE
Islands on the life line denote periods of low energy. Islands at the beginning are associated with respiratory disorders. Nearer the wrist, islands suggest a weakened constitution.

TRAUMA LINE
Bars cutting through the life line represent emotional upheaval. The longer the bar, the greater the impact of the event.

KERATOSES
Keratoses are lumps of hard skin often caused by friction. Occasionally they may point to organ disease. Located here may suggest kidney complaints.

DIAMOND
A large diamond attached to the life line about one-third of the way up the palm denotes possible gynecological problems in women or, in a man's hand urological disorders.

HUMPED RASCETTE
It has been observed that if, in a woman's hand, the top rascette arches steeply up into her palm, she may have a susceptibility to certain gynecological weaknesses, in particular experiencing difficulties when giving birth.

TASSELING
Fraying or tasseling of either the head or life lines reveals a dissipation of energy. If present, this is more likely to occur at the end of the line.

MORE CLUES TO YOUR HEALTH

OUR HANDS MIRROR the state of our cardiovascular system and therefore give vital information about the health of our circulation and general constitution. Abnormal color or temperature are key factors that aid diagnosis of a variety of diseases. The color and overall condition of the nails are also linked with specific illnesses, which may be either physical or psychological in origin.

THE FINGERNAILS

OUR NAILS ARE continually growing. Consequently, any changes in the blood supply to the nails will interfere with their development and mark them in some way. These fingernail markings give clues about our health.

SPECKLES
Speckling with white or gray flecks can be caused by periods of tiredness and stress. This is also believed to be a sign of an imbalance of zinc in the system.

VERTICAL RIDGES
Ribs from cuticle to tip, giving the nail a heavily ridged appearance, are associated with intestinal problems, such as colitis, or rheumatic conditions.

HORIZONTAL RIDGES
Also called Beau's lines, these grooves are caused by a trauma such as a bout of illness, an emotional upheaval, or a sudden reduction of dietary nutrients.

WRAPAROUND
Often found in the hands of smokers, nails that curve over the fingertip point to respiratory problems. When good health is restored the nails grow in a straight manner once more.

CONVEX
Convex nails dip in the center and the nail tip curls upward, away from the finger. This is associated with nutritional deficiencies such as anemia, or with thyroid problems.

FAN-SHAPED
People whose nails are fan-shaped tend to be somewhat high-strung. Prolonged stress can cause nails to take this shape, and they are a warning to the owner of the need to relax.

THE COLOR AND TEMPERATURE OF THE HANDS

COLOR AND TEMPERATURE often go together because both are determined by the circulation, but it is important that ambient temperature and recent activity are considered. Hot hands are to be expected after an aerobics class, but not after sitting quietly for half an hour.

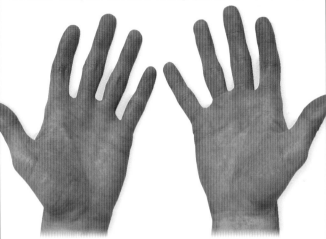

VERY RED HANDS
Hot, red hands and nails are associated with feverish conditions, with a rise in blood pressure, or with rheumatic conditions. Traditionally linked to an angry disposition, red hands are said to describe a volatile and irascible temperament. Physiologically, they may signify glandular, liver, or gout-type problems. In a woman's hand, a reddish blush over the percussion can be an early indication of pregnancy.

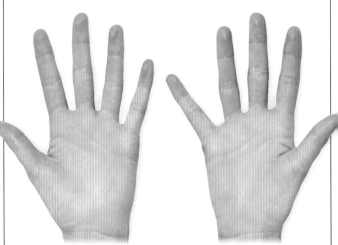

VERY PALE HANDS
Cold, pale hands and nails are linked to anemia. A temporary loss of iron after menstruation may be seen by the main lines appearing white when the hand is stretched out. Listlessness often accompanies the pale hand. Shock can immediately drain hands of color, or sometimes turn the hand blue. A prolonged bluish tinge of the skin or nails, known as cyanosis, should be investigated because it may denote circulatory or respiratory problems.

A HAND WORKOUT

MASSAGE IS NOW WIDELY accepted as a useful therapy for the relief of pain, promoting well-being and soothing or stimulating the body's responses.

Combining the principles behind the therapies of shiatsu and reflexology, a regular hand massage can help to keep your system and circulation toned.

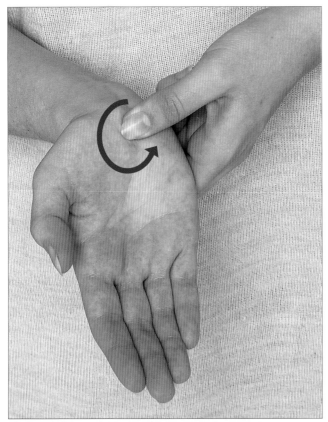

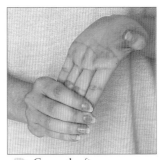

2 Grasp the fingers firmly and pull them downward until you feel tension at the wrist. Don't force your joints if you suffer from a rheumatic condition.

3 Slide your thumb tip between the tendons on the back of your hand. Press fairly firmly as you move from the web between the fingers up toward the wrist.

4 Pinch and rub the webs between the digits, paying special attention to the web between the thumb and the Jupiter finger. This action will dispel stored toxins.

5 With circular movements, pinch and rub the tip of each digit, including the thumb, first from side to side and then from front to back.

1 Use firm pressure when massaging the hands. Pressing down stimulates the circulation; stroking has a more relaxing effect. The movements of massage are always made toward the heart. Working on one hand at a time, begin by pressing your thumb tip in circular movements across the base of the hand. This loosens the muscles and ligaments.

6 Resting the back of one hand on the fingers of the other, begin massaging the palm, moving firmly across from one side to the other with the thumb.

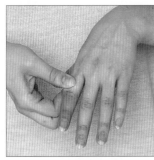

7 With the same movement, massage each finger working from the tip down, palm side first, then the backs. Remember to massage the thumb, too.

8 When you have finished the sequence on both hands, interlace the fingers and stretch the hands against each other, feeling the tension at the base of the digits.

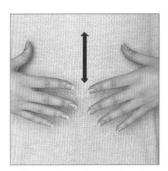

9 Finally, rub your hands together, stretch and flex the fingers as if you were throwing a ball, then shake your hands vigorously until they tingle.

MONEY AND LUCK

ONEY AND LUCK are often thought to be closely related, but in the art of hand analysis the two need to be teased apart and considered separately. Essentially, the construction of our hands reveals our attitudes toward wealth. For example, well-padded hands belong to people who are prepared to work hard for their living, whereas doughy hands reveal a lazy attitude and belong to people who enjoy the good life but are not prepared to work hard to achieve it. Luck is much more specific and may be picked out by well-defined markings in the palm.

THE FOUR HAND SHAPES

EACH OF THE FOUR CATEGORIES responds differently to the acquisition of money and accumulation of wealth. The lines and markings in our hands will track our individual financial situation through our lives, but the shape of our hands reveals our attitude toward money and how we are likely to handle our finances.

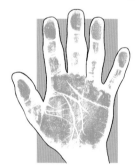

THE EARTH HAND
Owners of the Earth hand make money slowly through their own hard work. Cautious and prudent, they tend to build up their savings steadily, putting a little aside on a regular basis until they have a nest egg safely tucked away.

THE AIR HAND
Air-handed people have commercial flair and are often knowledgeable about the current state of the financial markets and investments. They happily move their money around to take advantage of deals.

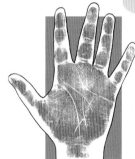

THE FIRE HAND
Through intuition or good fortune, Fire-handed people tend to attract money, although the supply of funds may be erratic. They do not like all their eggs in one basket and are inclined to speculate and invest their capital widely.

THE WATER HAND
Water hands are not remotely materialistic, neither business-minded nor financially oriented. They prefer to enrich their souls rather than their bank balances. However, their creative talents can make them very wealthy.

SIGNS OF THE RISK-TAKER

THE DESCRIPTION of spendthrifts as people whose money slips through their fingers is borne out by hand analysis. Our fingers reveal a great deal of information about money management. A straight Jupiter finger, for example, shows integrity and good sense. One that leans out toward the thumb hints at a thrill of adventure, and its owner would enjoy playing the markets. A Jupiter finger leaning toward the Saturn finger suggests a more cautious nature, and if the two fingers are held close together their owner would take no risks where their capital is concerned. A short Saturn finger shows untrustworthiness and irresponsibility in financial affairs.

LONG MIDDLE PHALANXES INDICATE EXCELLENT MANAGERIAL AND FINANCIAL SKILLS

LONG APOLLO FINGER DENOTES THE RISK-TAKER

THE GAMBLER'S HAND
A long Apollo finger, especially one that is longer than the Saturn finger, is the sign of a gambler. Other elements in the hand will show whether the risks are calculated or foolhardy. This hand reveals a shrewd dealer.

ELEGANT, LONG THUMB REVEALS ABILITY TO CALCULATE THE ODDS AND CONTROL IMPULSIVENESS

FORTUNE IN THE HAND

OF ALL THE LINES and markings that represent success, the star is the most outstanding omen of luck and good fortune but only – and this is most important – when it is found on the upper mounts of Jupiter, Apollo, or Mercury, at the top of the fate line or at any point along the Apollo line.

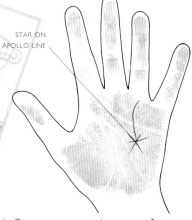

STAR ON JUPITER MOUNT

STAR ON APOLLO MOUNT

STAR ON APOLLO LINE

A STAR ON THE JUPITER MOUNT
Perhaps one of the most favorable positions in which to find a star is on the Jupiter mount, because here it highlights success that is accompanied by financial rewards. This person enjoyed good fortune, married advantageously, and reached a position of prestige in life.

A STAR ON THE APOLLO MOUNT
Standing independently on the Apollo mount, a star reveals extraordinary talents that are highly likely to bring its owner fame and fortune. It is generally acknowledged that in this position, the star is a mark of creative brilliance. In this case, the owner is a well-known actor.

A STAR ON THE APOLLO LINE
The freestanding star represents talents that bring their owner success, but a star attached to the Apollo line pinpoints a specific event of spectacular luck. Here, the star predicts a lottery win, and the consequent growth of the line denotes the happiness such a windfall brings.

AUSPICES AND WARNINGS

THE LINES IN OUR HANDS pinpoint our financial successes and failures, and the lucky breaks and downturns of fortune that are likely to occur throughout our lives. Our life line shows whether we possess strength and vitality sufficient to pursue our ambitions, and our head line reveals our business skills and talents for making money. However, our fate and Apollo lines chart our progress, highlighting when we may expect increases in salary, legacies, or windfalls. These lines can also warn us about potential pitfalls – for example, when, through bad luck or poor judgment, we are likely to encounter reversals in our fortunes. We can use these warnings to prepare ourselves to deal with financial problems.

CASE HISTORY
If this woman had consulted her hand before taking out a bank loan to expand her catering business, she would have seen that a large island on her fate line warned of trouble ahead. When she was 39, the business collapsed, leaving her in financial difficulties lasting for eight years. At the age of 47, a large square shows that, through hard work, she was able to rebuild her business. The new strong section of fate line above, and the strengthening of the Apollo lines above the heart line, confirm that by the age of 54 she was once again at the head of a successful company.

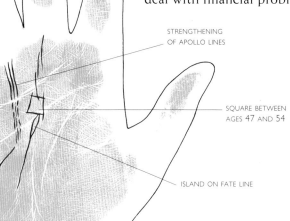

STRENGTHENING OF APOLLO LINES

SQUARE BETWEEN AGES 47 AND 54

ISLAND ON FATE LINE

TRAVEL AND MOVEMENT

TRAVEL BROADENS THE MIND, it is said, but it also leaves its mark on the hand. If the journey makes a lasting impression on the mind, it will also leave a corresponding impression engraved in the palm. Any journey will make an impression – from moving to a new house to long-distance travel. The markings that represent travel and movement are found in different locations on the hand according to the type of journey. Voyages of discovery, for instance, are the travel lines found across the percussion, while branches sweeping out from the life line denote relocation.

THE FOUR HAND SHAPES

SOME PEOPLE SEEM TO BE BORN with itchy feet, becoming restless if they remain in the same location for any length of time. Others are content to stay in familiar places. Although the lines individualize each person's pattern of movement, hand shape reveals attitudes toward travel and changes of environment.

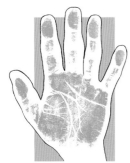

THE EARTH HAND
Earth-handed people like routine and tend to return to places they know and love. They are happy puttering around in the garden, but if they go on vacation they like to be outdoors and head for the country rather than the town.

THE AIR HAND
Air hands need variety and enjoy communicating with others. They derive immense stimulation and satisfaction from visiting foreign countries, and the travel industry is heavily populated by members of this group.

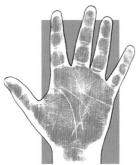

THE FIRE HAND
People with the Fire hand are great adventurers. They take to the open road with a childlike excitement, enjoying the thought of the uncharted territory, and the delights of the unfamiliar customs and cultures that lie ahead.

THE WATER HAND
Water-handed people seek communion in their travels, and enjoy cultural events, music festivals, and places of antiquity or historical interest. They are also drawn to the mystical, to shrines of peace, and locations of spiritual power.

CASE HISTORY

ROBIN HANBURY-TENISON has been on over two dozen major expeditions and has traveled extensively throughout the world. He has crossed the Sahara by camel, ridden along the Great Wall of China on horseback, lived among the tribes people of Amazonas, and studied the rain forests of Sarawak in Borneo. In his hand are all the signs indicative of a successful explorer – driving ambition in the long thumb and a wide-spaced Jupiter finger, courage in the huge mount of Mars positive, an indomitable spirit in the large Venus mount, breadth of vision in the well-developed percussion and low-placed mount of Luna, and last, but not least, the plethora of travel lines that are scored across his percussion.

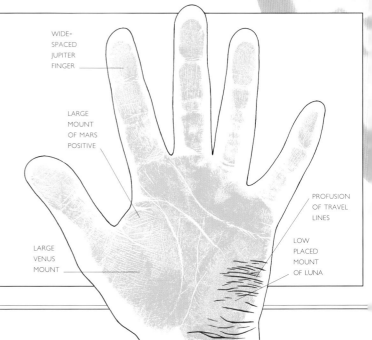

WIDE-SPACED JUPITER FINGER

LARGE MOUNT OF MARS POSITIVE

LARGE VENUS MOUNT

PROFUSION OF TRAVEL LINES

LOW PLACED MOUNT OF LUNA

RELOCATION

RELOCATING YOURSELF and your family is a landmark in your life, whether it is merely a move to a new house just a few streets away or a completely fresh start in a new country where you know no one. These important events will be registered in the hand, although the type of relocation will determine the way in which it is represented.

MOVING ABROAD

The Luna mount is associated with movement abroad, therefore a long journey, or a foreign relocation will be marked here. This woman's medical condition required her to move to a warm climate. Her subsequent emigration from England to America is shown by a branch from her life line, which shoots out to the Luna mount.

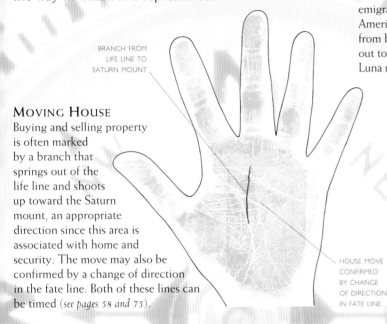

BRANCH FROM
LIFE LINE TO
SATURN MOUNT

MOVING HOUSE

Buying and selling property is often marked by a branch that springs out of the life line and shoots up toward the Saturn mount, an appropriate direction since this area is associated with home and security. The move may also be confirmed by a change of direction in the fate line. Both of these lines can be timed (*see pages 58 and 75*).

HOUSE MOVE
CONFIRMED
BY CHANGE
OF DIRECTION
IN FATE LINE

BREAK IN FATE
LINE DENOTES
START OF
NEW LIFE

ISLAND ON LIFE
LINE SHOWS
POOR HEALTH

BRANCH
FROM LIFE
LINE TO
LUNA
MOUNT

TRAVEL PROBLEMS

IN THE SAME WAY that the appearance of islands or stars on the major lines warns of potential problems in whatever aspect of life the line represents, negative markings on the travel lines across the percussion edge of the Luna mount will alert the traveler to possible hitches or complications while on their journeys.

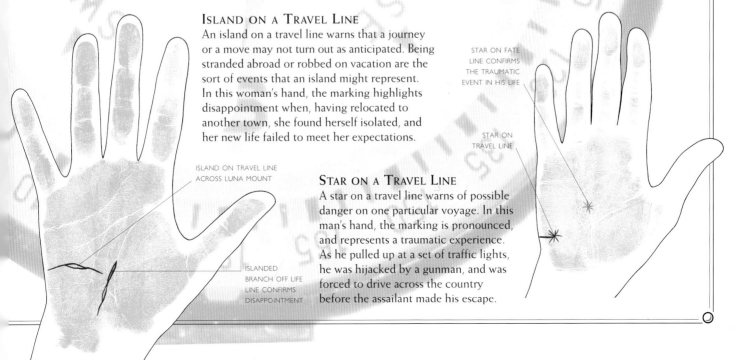

ISLAND ON A TRAVEL LINE

An island on a travel line warns that a journey or a move may not turn out as anticipated. Being stranded abroad or robbed on vacation are the sort of events that an island might represent. In this woman's hand, the marking highlights disappointment when, having relocated to another town, she found herself isolated, and her new life failed to meet her expectations.

ISLAND ON TRAVEL LINE
ACROSS LUNA MOUNT

ISLANDED
BRANCH OFF LIFE
LINE CONFIRMS
DISAPPOINTMENT

STAR ON FATE
LINE CONFIRMS
THE TRAUMATIC
EVENT IN HIS LIFE

STAR ON
TRAVEL LINE

STAR ON A TRAVEL LINE

A star on a travel line warns of possible danger on one particular voyage. In this man's hand, the marking is pronounced, and represents a traumatic experience. As he pulled up at a set of traffic lights, he was hijacked by a gunman, and was forced to drive across the country before the assailant made his escape.

RETIREMENT

SOME PEOPLE CONSIDER retirement to be a golden age, a time when they can do the things that busy lives and responsibilities prohibited throughout their careers. Other people dread giving up work because their job guarantees income, supplies instant camaraderie, and, perhaps most critical of all, provides status and identity. Whichever stance you take, ensuring a happy retirement requires careful planning, with domestic and financial provisions worked out in advance. Hand analysis can help you to understand your needs and smooth the transition.

THE FOUR HAND SHAPES

THE FOUR BASIC HAND SHAPES give a general picture of how each person approaches life. This provides an indication of the way they are likely to view the prospect of retirement. Hand shape will also suggest how someone is going to cope with the new and challenging demands of this stage in life.

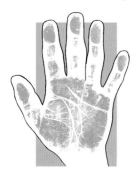

THE EARTH HAND
Of the four groups, the Earth hand finds retirement the most difficult. These people spend their lives working to established patterns, and are discomfited by changes in routine. However, time spent in the open air brings great satisfaction.

THE AIR HAND
When they retire, Air-handed people miss the buzz of a working environment and lose the opportunity to exchange news with their colleagues. Keeping in touch with friends and taking classes will bring them much pleasure.

THE FIRE HAND
People are important to Fire hands, and on retirement they miss their network of acquaintances. Naturally drawn to groups, the Fire hand will find fulfillment in joining clubs, community projects, or doing volunteer work for charity.

THE WATER HAND
Retirement holds the greatest pleasure for Water hands. They feel liberated from the hurly-burly of daily work, and happily fill their days with art and music, reading or writing poetry, and developing their creative skills.

A FRESH START

AN INESCAPABLE PART of our retirement years is bereavement and, while it is neither possible nor morally justifiable to predict an individual's death from the markings in the hand alone, it is possible to detect anxiety over the health and well-being of a close partner. In this woman's hand, a line originates high on the percussion and drops down to meet a large island on the fate line. This corresponds to a difficult period in her life during which her husband became ill and passed away. The subsequent break in the fate line and development, five years later, of a strong, new section of line represents fresh beginnings. Also, at the same time as the fate line grows, the Apollo line strengthens, suggesting newfound happiness and love.

APOLLO LINE
IS STRONGER

ISLAND AND
ORIGINAL FATE
LINE COME
TO AN END

STRONG
NEW
SECTION OF
FATE LINE

LINE HIGH ON
PERCUSSION

A NEW LIFE
This woman's hand holds hopeful signs for the future.

LARGE
ISLAND
ON FATE
LINE

RETIREMENT IN THE LINES

THE QUALITY OF YOUR RETIREMENT years is represented by the topmost sections of the fate and Apollo lines, and the end of the life line. Information here will alert you when to expect change, watch for health or financial problems, start new projects, or enhance those aspects that will most enrich your life.

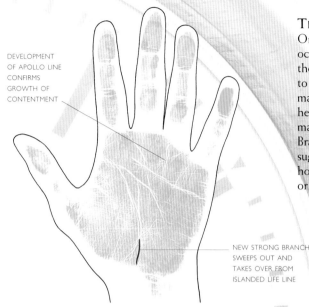

DEVELOPMENT OF APOLLO LINE CONFIRMS GROWTH OF CONTENTMENT

NEW SECTION OF FATE LINE SIGNIFIES EARLY RETIREMENT

THE END OF THE FATE LINE
On retirement, changes usually occur in the fate line, representing the transition from public life to private life. The line may make a clean break, as shown here. Alternatively, the break may overlap or change direction. Branches or multiples of the line suggest expansion of interest. Islands, however, warn of financial problems or dissatisfaction.

NEW STRONG BRANCH SWEEPS OUT AND TAKES OVER FROM ISLANDED LIFE LINE

DEVELOPMENT OF APOLLO LINE AT SAME TIME AS RETIREMENT BEGINS

THE END OF THE LIFE LINE
Approximately the last two-fifths of the life line correspond to the retirement years. If this section is unblemished, vitality can be expected. Islands suggest bouts of poor health, while branches sweeping out represent journeys. In this woman's hand, a strong new branch takes over from a weak life line, showing that retirement has improved the quality of her life.

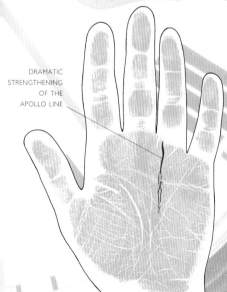

DRAMATIC STRENGTHENING OF THE APOLLO LINE

APOLLO LINE ABOVE THE HEART LINE
In many hands, the Apollo line occurs only above the heart line, auguring a contented old age, especially if the line is strong and well-formed. Three parallel lines, as in this hand, have a traditional interpretation concerning finances. Although this marking does not imply unimaginable riches, it certainly suggests that there will be enough money to get by.

THREE APOLLO LINES ABOVE HEART LINE

THE ENDING OF THE APOLLO LINE
Retirement is the time when we can pursue personal goals, and the Apollo line, representing personal happiness, will show the degree of fulfillment achieved. Here, from midpalm upward, the line is fragmented, revealing disappointments during the person's 30s and 40s. However, the strengthening of the Apollo line above the heart line shows contentment during later years.

GROWTH AND CHANGE

HAND ANALYSIS ENABLES us not only to gather information about our character, potential, talents, and genetic inheritance, but also to monitor the development and progress of our lives – to keep tabs on what is affecting and happening to us and our loved ones. It is very important to remember that the lines in our hands can and do change, and that our markings represent only possibility, not irrevocable absolutes. Our hands offer us pointers about future direction or early warnings concerning potential problems ahead. We have free will, and can interpret these signs and act upon them, and take whatever action is necessary to avoid troubles in the future.

DEVELOPMENT OF THE LINES

THE SHAPE OF OUR HANDS and the lines and markings in our palms change and grow throughout our lives. Our decisions, knowledge, and the influences that shape us, and changes of attitudes, environment, lifestyle, and even of diet can all affect the course of our lives and, by implication, the development of our lines.

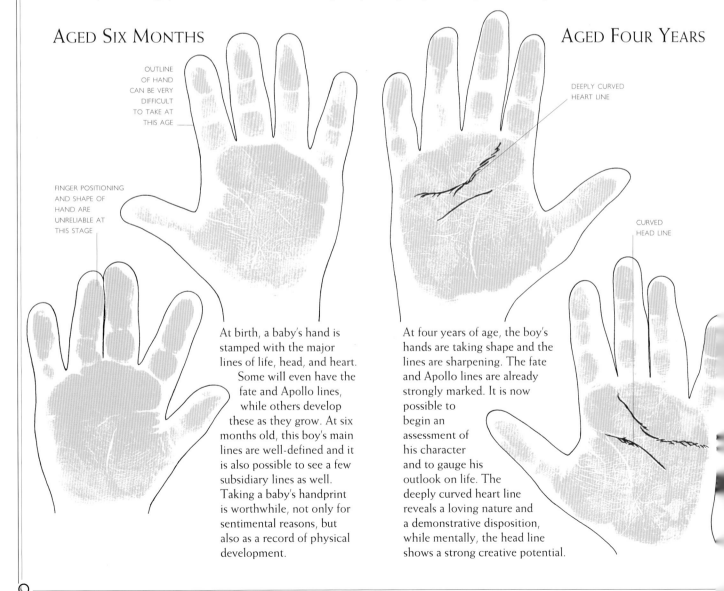

AGED SIX MONTHS

OUTLINE OF HAND CAN BE VERY DIFFICULT TO TAKE AT THIS AGE

FINGER POSITIONING AND SHAPE OF HAND ARE UNRELIABLE AT THIS STAGE

At birth, a baby's hand is stamped with the major lines of life, head, and heart. Some will even have the fate and Apollo lines, while others develop these as they grow. At six months old, this boy's main lines are well-defined and it is also possible to see a few subsidiary lines as well. Taking a baby's handprint is worthwhile, not only for sentimental reasons, but also as a record of physical development.

AGED FOUR YEARS

DEEPLY CURVED HEART LINE

CURVED HEAD LINE

At four years of age, the boy's hands are taking shape and the lines are sharpening. The fate and Apollo lines are already strongly marked. It is now possible to begin an assessment of his character and to gauge his outlook on life. The deeply curved heart line reveals a loving nature and a demonstrative disposition, while mentally, the head line shows a strong creative potential.

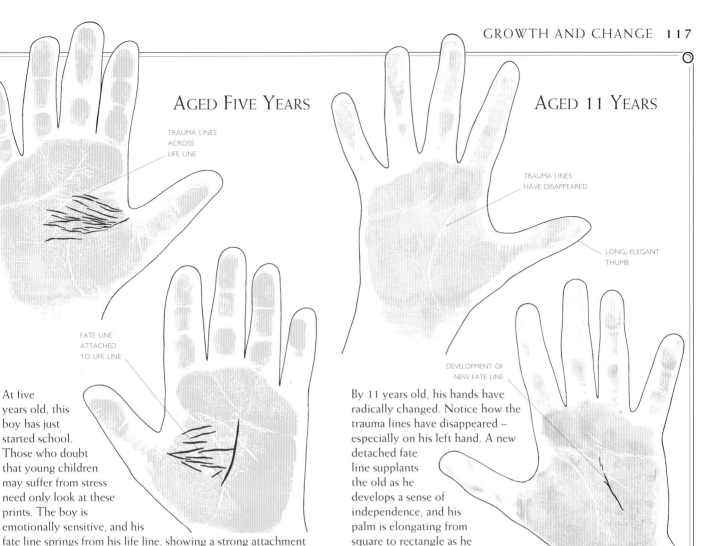

AGED FIVE YEARS

TRAUMA LINES
ACROSS
LIFE LINE

FATE LINE
ATTACHED
TO LIFE LINE

At five
years old, this
boy has just
started school.
Those who doubt
that young children
may suffer from stress
need only look at these
prints. The boy is
emotionally sensitive, and his
fate line springs from his life line, showing a strong attachment
to home and family. He finds the separation from his parents
deeply painful, and the plethora of trauma lines across his life
line, even at this tender age, reveal the extent of his anxiety.

AGED 11 YEARS

TRAUMA LINES
HAVE DISAPPEARED

LONG, ELEGANT
THUMB

DEVELOPMENT OF
NEW FATE LINE

By 11 years old, his hands have
radically changed. Notice how the
trauma lines have disappeared –
especially on his left hand. A new
detached fate
line supplants
the old as he
develops a sense of
independence, and his
palm is elongating from
square to rectangle as he
becomes more studious. The long,
slender thumbs denote elegance of
expression and decisiveness.

Electronic Palm Print Recognition

MODERN TECHNOLOGICAL ADVANCES HAVE
REVOLUTIONIZED THE USE OF PALMAR SKIN PATTERNS IN
THE FIELD OF PERSONAL IDENTIFICATION.

———— • ————

SOPHISTICATED TECHNIQUES in criminal detection employ automatic
fingerprinting recognition systems (AFR), which store, match, and
retrieve fingerprints in seconds. However, recognition
of hand and fingerprints has an even wider applicability for the
identification of personnel. Several systems employing laser
scanners to image and computerize handprints are currently under
development. These digitized images may be transferred onto
"smart cards" and used, for example, on swipe cards to activate
entrance commands into buildings and other areas.

HANDS ON
*Pioneering systems, using sensitivity pads to scan and match
handprints of regular passengers, are already in operation in
some of the world's busiest international airports.*

GLOSSARY

- **AIR HAND** A hand type comprising square palm and long fingers.
- **ALLERGY LINE** *see Via Lascivia.*
- **ANGLE OF MANUAL DEXTERITY** The second joint of the thumb is prominent, denoting excellent manual skills.
- **ANGLE OF TIMING** The bottom joint of the thumb is prominent, denoting musical ability.
- **APOLLO FINGER** The ring or third finger, associated with creativity and personal satisfaction.
- **APOLLO LINE** Ending on the Apollo mount, this line reveals creativity and happiness.
- **APOLLO MOUNT** Located beneath the Apollo finger, it determines the potential for fame and fortune.
- **ARCH** A fingerprint pattern that appears in the form of either gentle or very curved arches. It denotes materialism and practicality.
- **BAR** A short line across a major line, representing opposition or obstruction.
- **BOW OF INTUITION** A secondary marking found on the percussion beneath the Mercury finger. It reveals acute powers of perception.
- **CHAIN** A series of islands on a line, giving a chainlike appearance. It signifies a reduction of energy in the area of life the line represents.
- **CHIROGNOMY** The traditional name for the study of the shape of the hand.
- **CHIROLOGY** The traditional name for the study of the hand, encompassing chirognomy and chiromancy.
- **CHIROMANCY** The study of the lines in the hand.
- **CLEAN BREAK** A break in a line, without overlapped ends, signifying enforced change.
- **COMPOSITE** A fingerprint pattern that comprises two loops pulling in opposite directions. It denotes open-mindedness.
- **CROSS** A marking that can appear on a mount or a line, it usually warns of opposition.
- **CURVED PERCUSSION** A palm with a markedly curved or bowed outside edge.

- **DOMINANT HAND** For right-handed people, the right hand; for left-handed people, the left hand.
- **EARTH HAND** A hand type comprising square palm and short fingers.
- **FATE LINE** A major line that runs up the palm. It charts career progress and responsibilities.
- **FIRE HAND** A hand type comprising rectangular palm and short fingers.
- **GIRDLE OF VENUS** A marking that straddles the roots of the Saturn and Apollo fingers. Its presence suggests hypersensitivity.
- **GRILLE** A marking that appears on the mounts and signifies heightened emotions and tension.
- **HEAD LINE** A major line that crosses the palm horizontally, representing the intellect.
- **HEART LINE** A major line that crosses the palm horizontally, representing the emotions.
- **ISLAND** An island is the temporary splitting of a line and denotes weakness, anxiety, or lack of energy for the period of its duration.
- **JUPITER FINGER** The index or first finger, associated with the ego, and personal standing in the world.
- **JUPITER MOUNT** The mount beneath the Jupiter finger. Its development reveals one's sense of self-worth and authority.
- **LIFE LINE** A major line that encircles the thumb, representing health and the quality of life.
- **LOOP** A fingerprint pattern that appears as a loop and can curve either toward the thumb (ulna), or away from the thumb (radial). Also may be found on the palm.
- **LUNA MOUNT** The mount at the base of the hand, on the percussion.
- **LUNULA** *see Moon.*
- **MAJOR LINES** The principal lines comprising the life line, heart line, head line, fate line, and Apollo line.
- **MARS LINE** A line that appears inside and parallel to the life line, giving secondary protection.
- **MARS NEGATIVE MOUNT** Located at the center of the percussion, above the Luna mount, this mount reveals integrity and endurance.

- **MARS POSITIVE MOUNT** Situated between the thumb and the Jupiter mount, this mount represents courage and/or aggression.
- **MERCURY FINGER** The little finger, it represents communication.
- **MERCURY LINE** A secondary line that, depending on where in the palm it begins, signifies health or business acumen.
- **MERCURY MOUNT** Below the Mercury finger, this mount reveals communication abilities.
- **MOON** The white crescent sometimes visible near the nail root. Also known as a lunula.
- **NEPTUNE MOUNT** Located at the base of the palm, between the Luna and Venus mounts.
- **OVERLAPPED BREAK** A break in a line where the new section takes over from the old and their two ends are overlapped. It signifies change brought about by choice.
- **PALMAR RIDGES** The corrugated surface of the skin on the palm that forms into patterns like fingerprints.
- **PASSIVE HAND** For a right-handed person, the left hand; for a left-handed person, the right hand.
- **PEACOCK'S EYE** A fingerprint pattern comprising a whorl enclosed in a loop. It confers protection.
- **PERCUSSION** The outside edge of the hand, opposite the thumb.
- **PHALANXES** The bones and sections of the fingers and thumbs.
- **PLAIN OF MARS** The flat area at the center of the palm, surrounded by the mounts.
- **RASCETTES** The lines or "bracelets" located at the top of the wrist. They are associated with health.
- **RIDGES** *see Palmar Ridges.*
- **RING OF APOLLO** A fairly unusual secondary marking that appears around the Apollo finger. It signifies a block to creativity.
- **RING OF SATURN** A secondary marking found at the base of the Saturn finger that denotes pessimism.
- **RING OF SOLOMON** A secondary marking around the base of the Jupiter finger symbolizing wisdom.
- **SATURN FINGER** The middle or second finger, associated with responsibility and security.

- **SATURN MOUNT** Located beneath the Saturn finger, this mount reveals the extent of introspection, but if overdeveloped can denote cynicism and melancholy.
- **SECONDARY LINES** Lines, other than the major lines, that may or may not appear on the hand.
- **SIMIAN LINE** A phenomenon where the head and heart line are merged. It denotes emotional intensity or a genetic anomaly.
- **SQUARE** A pattern that signifies protection, except when it appears on the Jupiter mount, where it denotes teaching ability.
- **STAR** A marking that can appear on a line or mount, representing either shock or achievement.
- **STRAIGHT PERCUSSION** The outside of the palm appears to be straight, from the wrist to the base of the Mercury finger.
- **SYDNEY LINE** A head line that travels right across the palm. It suggests hyperactivity.
- **TAPERED PERCUSSION** The outside of the palm curves out beneath the Mercury finger, then narrows toward the wrist.
- **TRAVEL LINES** Lines that are found across the base of the percussion representing journeys.
- **TRI-RADII** A triangular formation of skin ridges formed at the meeting point of three sets of skin ridge patterns.
- **TRIANGLE** A marking that appears on the mounts and signifies success accompanied by wisdom.
- **VENUS MOUNT** The mount at the base of the thumb, symbolizing vitality and sexuality.
- **VIA LASCIVIA** A line appearing across the base of the percussion. Its presence suggests sensitivity to foods and chemicals. Also known as the allergy line.
- **WATER HAND** A hand type comprising rectangular palm and long fingers.
- **WHORLS** A skin pattern that appears on the fingertips and the palm. It denotes fixed attitudes.
- **ZONES** Divisions of the hand, each of which represents a different aspect of the character.

INDEX

ACKNOWLEDGMENTS

ARTWORKS
Anatomical illustrations by Philip Wilson
Computer illustrations by Ken McMahon of Pelican Graphics
Line illustrations by Will Giles and Sandra Pond

LINE WORK
Karen Cochrane and Stephen Dew

SPECIAL PHOTOGRAPHY
Andy Crawford, Steve Gorton, Garry Ombler, Dave King
Photographic retouching by Ken McMahon of Pelican Graphics

ADDITIONAL PHOTOGRAPHY
Paul Bricknell, Gordon Clayton, Philip Gatward,
Barnabus Kindersley, Stephen Oliver, Matthew Ward

JACKET DESIGN
Neal Cobourne

INDEXER
Karin Woodruff

EDITORIAL ADVICE
Sharon Lucas

PICTURE RESEARCHER
Christine Rista

PRINCIPAL HAND MODEL: Kirsty Ashton Bell
THANKS ALSO TO:
Zirrina Austin, Anna Benjamin, Andy Crawford, Mark Davis,
Ursula Dawson, Carla De Abreu, Steve Gorton,
Angela Marie Graham, Paul Greenleaf, Tracy Hambleton-Miles,
Phil Hunt, Stephen Josland, Peter Kindersley, Laura Langley,
Tracie Lee, Sarah Lillicrapp, Anna Lord, Sharon Lucas,
Krystyna Mayer, Daniel McCarthy, Annabel Morgan,
Rachael Parfitt, Marianne Petrou, Gurinder Purewall,
Nerina Ramcharran, James Rankin, Tim Ridley,
Kevin Ryan, Jane Sarluis, Tim Scott,
Tracey Strudwick, Martha Swift,
Harjinder Singh Tattal, Amanda Tomeh,
Alison Verity, Jo Walton

PICTURE CREDITS
The publisher would like to thank the following for their
kind permission to reproduce their photographs:
t: top; c: centre; b: below; l: left; r: right.
ADVERTISING ARCHIVES: 17tl; BRIDGEMAN ART LIBRARY: 83bl,
/Galleria dell' Accademia, Venice 10b, Hever Castle Ltd. 37br,
Lambeth Palace Library, London 18tr, Phillips Auctioneers 49cl,
Pinacoteca Capitolina, Palazzo Conservatori, Rome 11bc,
Vatican Museum and Galleries, Rome 17bl; BRUCE COLEMAN:
Stefano Amantini 15br, John Concalosi 10t, Christian Zuber
61bc; MARY EVANS PICTURE LIBRARY: 19tl; IMAGE SELECT: Ann
Ronan Collection 14tr, 68cl; IMAGES COLOUR LIBRARY: 12tr, 12bl,
13tr, 13bl, 14bl, 56cl, 62cl, 71tl, 73tr, 97tr; POPPERFOTO: 16tr,
19br; REX FEATURES: 28bl, 42tr, 79tr, 81tl, /Nils Jorgensen 93cl,
98bl, Philip Reeve 45br, Sten Rosenlund 27br, SCL 98br, Sipa
Press 16bl, 17tr, 28bc, Today 29br; SCIENCE PHOTO LIBRARY:
Peter Menzel 47br, Petit Format/Nestle 27bc, Philippe Plailly
117br; SOUTH AMERICAN PICTURES: Tony Morrison 65tr;
UNIVERSITY COLLEGE LONDON: 61bl.

Jacket, front cover: all pictures Dorling Kindersley.
Jacket, back cover: BRUCE COLEMAN: John Cancalosi tl;
IMAGES COLOUR LIBRARY: tr, cr, bl; Dorling Kindersley: cl.
Jacket borders: IMAGES COLOUR LIBRARY.

AUTHOR'S ACKNOWLEDGMENTS
I am indebted to Stephen Carter for advice on shiatsu; Graham
Hughes, FFS, for so kindly giving his valuable time to keep me
up to date on the latest forensic technology; Philip Wilson for his
detailed and impeccable anatomical drawings; Kevin Ryan for his
patience and forbearance and his brilliant artistic insight; Tracie
Lee for so perfectly coming to grips with this complex subject
and for her uncanny ability to read between the lines;
David Lamb for keeping the flame alive and backing
me all the way; my clients and all those who have
enthusiastically contributed their handprints;
and especially to my friends and family for
so willingly stepping in whenever I needed
"just one more print."

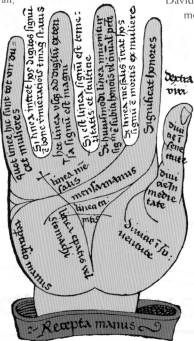